The church every church planter needs

COMPILED BY LEE STEPHENSON

The Church Every Church Planter Needs
© 2019 Converge

Published by Converge
2002 S. Arlington Heights Rd.
Arlington Heights, IL 60005
converge.org

Print ISBN 978-0-578-58140-8
Digital ISBN 978-0-578-58159-0
Library of Congress Control Number: 2019914546

Printed in the United States of America

Compiled by Lee Stephenson
Editing team: Lee Stephenson, Joshua Young, Mickey Seward, Michael Smith
Designed by Ryan Emenecker

 CONVERGE   START. STRENGTHEN. SEND.

Dedicated to the churches and individuals that **RISK BIG** to see the **KINGDOM GROW.**

Contents

Foreword

ED STETZER

Not too long ago, I was scrolling through Twitter and ran across a story that received some traction when a host of people reposted it. The story was about how a pastor candidate didn't receive a "super" majority vote. It reminded me how our Christian culture today tends to fixate on the kind of pastor that a church needs.

Don't get me wrong; I can see why there is so much focus on the kind of pastor that a local church needs. Amid the new stories of pastor fatigue, burnout and moral failings, churches want to make sure the pastor meets the church's biblical qualifications and fits its culture. In addition, with such a rapidly changing cultural milieu, churches want a pastor who can help them culturally navigate such a climate in a manner that keeps them rooted, yet relevant. Thus, I totally understand the importance of such conversations.

But shouldn't this focus be more balanced? What about pastors? What kind of churches do pastors need? While I believe there are certain biblical qualifications and expectations assigned to pastors, I also believe there are biblical expectations outlined for congregations as to the kind of body they are to be for their pastors. For instance, churches should be about *koinonia,* unity, shared leadership and service. They should be bodies ready to submit to, learn from, care for, honor, protect and encourage their leaders.

I think something similar has transpired with church planting. There's been a lot of focus on the kind of planters needed for successful church planting today. With a rise in denominational focus toward church planting, in addition to the creation and evolution of church planting networks, to the formation of local church planting residencies in churches throughout the U.S., there's been a lot of focus on the kind of church planters needed today.

Again, don't get me wrong; I think this is a good thing. However, there still remains a significant gap in established churches being involved in church planting. This is why I believe my good friend Lee Stephenson's compiled work is so helpful in this conversation. This book offers a more balanced approach, as the authors help us think about what kind of church a church planter needs.

I cannot tell you how often I hear denominational and network leaders express difficulty in finding quality planters. But whose fault is it that we have a shortage of planters? Does it lie in individuals not stepping up to answer the call? Or could it be that the primary location where planters should be found (e.g., local churches) aren't necessarily conducive environments in producing church planters? I believe every local church, regardless of size, has — as an old country preacher once said — "gold in them there pews." Therefore, every local church has gold ready to be mined.

The question at hand then is, how does a local church become that body that not only cultivates church planters but is that kind of church that a planter needs?

Through this compiled work, the authors take us on a personal journey describing the characteristics that church planters need from local sending and parenting congregations.

I can attest that every one of these authors, all from within Converge, speaks as faithful and authoritative practitioners. Over the years, having worked closely with a lot of denominational and network entities on church planting, I can honestly say that the leaders at Converge know church planting.

Maybe you're a pastor of a church that is already engaged in church planting and you need a sounding board to make sure you're on the right track. This book is for you. Or, maybe you're a pastor, and you and a body of leaders are wanting to lead your church toward church planting, but you don't know where to start. You might feel more like you are winging it. It's like you are trying to sing karaoke to a song you don't know. And rather than being confident about what it will take to invest in a church plant and planter, you're bobbing your head and going through the motions. Don't worry; this book is a great guide.

The truth is, every church should engage at some level in church planting. Every church can play a role in being the kind of church every church planter needs.

I think this statement from Lee cuts at the heart of the book, "[Church planters] need local church pastors and leaders to understand why church planting matters, and then engage with it. Church planters need your wisdom, your experience, your structures and your support in order to thrive."

In closing, my exhortation to established churches — regardless of size — planters need you! So let Lee and the team be your guide for becoming the kind of church that planters need. Enjoy.

Why church planting matters

LEE STEPHENSON

Lead Pastor of Harvest Community Church
& Executive Director of Church Planting, Converge

In the first week of February 2004, I walked into a graduate course that changed the trajectory of my life.

For six years I had been a youth pastor in South Bend, Indiana. That winter I walked into a class simply to fulfill an elective requirement to finish my master's degree. I opted to take a church planting multiplication class because my mind was more on the multiplication side (for my current role) than church planting. In fact, church planting was something that was completely foreign to me. But on the first day of class the professor said something that changed my life:

"The most effective way to reach people for Jesus is to start new churches."

Something about that phrase, at that moment in my life, and through the power of the Holy Spirit, struck me to the core. A holy discontent rose up within me, and I knew in that snowy February morning class that the next season of my life would be dedicated to church planting. I would give my life for this.

In May of that same year, my wife, Melissa, and I accepted a call to move to Arizona to join the staff team of a church that had a dream to eventually plant a church, but also needed some help locally in their current ministry. We gave our time to them with the agreement that we would not be at that church for longer than five years. Over the course of those five years, we started a college age ministry, a young adults ministry and a young married ministry. We saw God move through incredible ways within this established church, honed our vision and strategy to begin a new work, and, almost five years to the day, we stepped out in faith to plant Harvest Community Church of Mesa, Arizona.

In those early days, I underestimated the difficulty and the pushback I would receive from other Christians and even Christian leaders. They would look at me puzzled as I would share our vision for a new church. Then, without provocation, they'd ask, "Why would you start a new church when so many of our existing churches have a need and are declining in impact?" They echoed what I have found to be two key objections to planting new churches: We don't have enough people or money to go around.

In his Ph.D. dissertation, Jeffery Farmer studied 624 established Baptist churches surrounding the topic of revitalization connected to church planting.[1] The averaged statistics he found within five years after an established church planted another church were shocking:

- Designated gifts increased by 77.4%.
- Undesignated tithes increased by 48.4%.
- Worship attendance increased by 21.5%.[2]

As we can see, Dr. Farmer's work directly addresses the two major concerns of many established churches, and this concrete research shows that churches directly benefit from planting new churches. The model of supply and demand fails to recognize some important underlying characteristics of God's kingdom economy.

God is ushering in a new way of life, bringing in a new Master and King over the world and through his people. This is called the kingdom of God. In God's kingdom, the first is last, the lowest place of humility is the highest place of honor, and when you steward what he has given you well, he gives you more.[3] These principles are in direct opposition to a supply-and-demand mentality that seems too often to squelch church planting imagination.

The stakes are too high to ignore. Inaction is not an option for the Christian and it is certainly not an option for the church. And we find when we begin to move out and plant new churches in faith, he increases his kingdom both in established churches and new churches.

This is why we must engage with the kingdom of God through church planting. There are many reasons to do this, but here are a few important arguments why church planting should be at the center of your church and ministry.

The kingdom of God is at stake

The very first command in the Bible is "be fruitful and multiply" (Gen. 1:22). From the beginning, God commanded all living things to reproduce, that is, "according to its kind." For lions that meant "reproduce lions." For plants that meant "reproduce plants." For Adam and Eve that meant "have lots of children."

Throughout the New Testament we see the church described as a living, active entity that's on the move.[4] Healthy families multiply. Most parents I know would not consider it a win if their 30-year-old son lives in the basement playing video games. Healthy ecosystems reproduce. So, just as everything that is alive will grow, mature and reproduce, the same is true for the church. A church reproduces itself by starting other churches. This is all a part of God's kingdom expansion. God is passionate about his rule and reign in the world, with the specific desire that his kingdom will encompass every community and every tribe — and will reach every person. One church cannot do this. Many churches can. Fred Herron adds to this thought in his book, *Expanding God's Kingdom through Church Planting*, when he states:

> "God intends the church to proclaim and demonstrate the kingdom so that his kingdom will spread to every people group on the earth. The passion in God's heart for the expansion of his kingdom is a desire for all nations to glorify God the eternal King. He has given the church a kingly commission to go into the entire world and make disciples who are loyal worshippers of the King. The heart of God for kingdom expansion is the foundation for planting new churches."[5]

We fulfill both the first command of Scripture and the Great Commission by multiplying churches. By planting churches, we take Jesus into the lives of needy people, we become partners with God's mission and we are actively expanding God's kingdom. God's heart beats for church planting and so should ours!

The commission of God is at stake

Jesus has given his church a specific Great Commission, and that directly involves the planting of new churches.

> "Go therefore and make disciples of all nations, baptizing them in the name of the Father and of the Son and of the Holy Spirit, teaching them to observe all that I have commanded you. And behold, I am with you always, to the end of the age." (Matt. 28:19-1:1)

Personal evangelism is paramount to fulfill the first portion of this commission. We need to GO and MAKE disciples. This has somewhat gotten lost in many of the churches in America. Somewhere along the way we decided it is OK for us to be believers and simply attend a sermon on Sunday, then go out and live our lives for ourselves. This is disobedience to God's call on our lives. But as believers share the gospel and disciples are made, they immediately become part of the global, universal, historical church.[6]

But, the command to baptize and teach extends beyond personal evangelism into the functions of a local church. Consistently in Acts we see people being baptized into a local expression of God's global church. As disciples are made, churches are formed.

So, the starting of new localized expressions of the global church is a critical component of the Great Commission. It provides the structure upon which a disciple can be a disciple and a sent one. Because of this, all of us are called to engage in it. And this is why C. Peter Wagner said, "Planting new churches is the most effective evangelistic methodology known under heaven."[7] New disciples by default will produce new churches over time. If you are a believer, the Great Commission is part of the calling on your life.

In other words, there is no such thing as a Christian who doesn't live on mission for the Lord and there is no advancement of the church without multiplication. The building of the church is a secondary but critical component of the Great Commission. What would it look like if new churches were born out of personal evangelism?

With this in mind, church planting becomes more than a novel idea. It comes with a sense of urgency. It is through the relentless planting of new churches that we see God's commission fulfilled in communities around the world that are under the reign of darkness.[8]

Community engagement is at stake
Planting churches is about reaching people for Jesus who seem-

ingly feel unreachable. The stark reality is that most "lost" people are best reached in a community that is similar and somewhat comfortable to them. This is true of groups separated by language, geography and even core identity. And we see this concept in a unique analogy within Paul's letter to the Corinthians:

> "Therefore, we are **ambassadors** for Christ, God making his appeal through us." (2 Cor. 5:20)

We are not simply messengers of the good news of Jesus (just telling), but we are ambassadors (living representatives) of God's kingdom.[9] This means that we need new kingdom outposts as embassies to train and deploy new kingdom ambassadors to live within the lost people of a specific community.

Statistically, new churches best reach the unchurched.

> "Dozens of denominational studies have confirmed that the average new church gains most of its new members (60-80%) from the ranks of people who are not attending any worshiping body, while churches over 10 to 15 years of age gain 80-90% of new members by transfer from other congregations."[10]

With this in mind, we start churches driven by biblical convictions of engaging people and communities who are far from God.

The compassion of Christ is at stake

> "When he saw the crowds, he had compassion for them, because they were harassed and helpless, like sheep without a shepherd." (Matt. 9:36)

Just over three years ago, my family and I arrived in Orlando eager to meet new people, figure out a new city and begin a new season of ministry. It would be dishonest of me to say that all the tears shed in our house during our transition have been tears of joy. The past three years have contained a wide range of emotions, from anxiety over health challenges to the joy of watching our son's baptism.

Recently, my wife, Melissa, began devoting time at a local Christian women's clinic. This clinic operates with the purpose to encourage and equip women and men to make informed pregnancy decisions. In other words, they hope to put all the local abortion clinics out of business. Our hearts were broken when we heard one of the abortion clinics in town was offering 50% off on late-term abortions. Once again it was a reminder that the world isn't the way it is supposed to be.

Two times in the Gospels we see Jesus cry. In John 11, we read about the death of Jesus' close friend, Lazarus. A few days after Lazarus' death, Jesus gathered together with his family and wept. This is strange, because the narrative goes on to explain that Jesus resurrected his friend from the dead. So it does not make sense that Jesus would cry over the death itself. Rather, Jesus cried as he gazed upon those who believed in him, yet still experienced the effects of the fall. In Luke 19, we read of Jesus weeping as he approached Jerusalem. He cried aloud in anguish over the unbelief of the city, knowing that its fate was a continued rejection of himself as Messiah.

The more we pursue Jesus, the more we become like the one who came to "seek and save the lost." To follow him is to embrace his commission, and his commission is an expression of deep love and compassion for the lost and those affected by the fall. Disciples are ones who have been captured by the love of Christ. This is why churches sacrifice financially, give their best leaders and go to forgotten places. People need Jesus, and there are communities all around us that are desperate to have a life-giving church in their community. Compassion is why we plant churches. Who is going to reach them if we don't? Who is going to weep for them if not us?

No matter what

If I am honest, I don't weep enough over my city, my community or my neighborhood. But, my prayer is that we will all feel the compassion of Jesus in greater ways to mourn with those who mourn. I pray we too will anguish over the lostness of those close to us. But then we must also go, seeing the rule and reign of Jesus' kingdom expand, committing to the Great Commission and engaging the lost as ambassadors being sent out from local churches.

Let our battle cry be, "No matter what!"

As we consider the unique role of church planting, I want to highlight that part of my story is how God used an existing church to encourage, foster and grow my call from simply an aspiration in graduate school into a beautiful reality. Those five years at Harvest Community Church saw lasting ministry that caused that local church to grow and helped develop my wife and I as leaders, which proved invaluable for Harvest to succeed. Church planting can be intricately connected and fostered within an already established church context, and it is statistically proven that churches who plant churches will actually grow in attendance themselves.

We need local church pastors and leaders to understand why church planting matters, and then engage with it. Church planters need your wisdom, your experience, your structures and your support in order to thrive. Planting a church will benefit your church, it will benefit the kingdom being advanced, it will contribute to the fulfillment of the Great Commission, it will allow for greater community engagement, and it will renew and revitalize your church's compassion for the lost.

The hope of the world is Jesus, and he chose the church to exist as his vehicle for achieving God's redemptive plan. If you believe this…we have work to do!

2

Interceding
for the
impossible

GLENN HERSCHBERGER

Executive Director of Church Planting,
Converge Great Lakes

I have vivid childhood memories of being captivated by the reports of missionaries that our church sent to faraway places. Usually, they would give presentations during a Sunday evening or midweek service. They would share stories of the great physical and spiritual needs of people in Russia, the Congo, the Philippines, and give names to the lost and hungry half a world away. These events were formative in my life, but the one thing that always stood out to me was these missionaries would always request prayer. Before asking for financial support, before the appeal to young men and women to come join them on the field (which they desperately needed), prayer was always their first priority.

When I entered into the world of church planting 20 years

ago, our family was advised to recruit 30-50 prayer partners to intercede for us on a regular basis. With the pressure of raising financial support and beginning to form new relationships to start a new work, it took discipline and time to form that prayer team as the priority goal amongst all the other things we had to accomplish. However, I can attest to the fruit we saw from it. Believers from other churches joined with us to pray for the abundance of the harvest and the successful launch of our new church. This helped established churches get excited about the vision God had given us. And as we met the people in our new community, they affirmed that they had been praying for a new church in their area for years before we arrived. Our brothers and sisters in Christ had been asking our Heavenly Father for exactly the same thing we were petitioning for, even before we knew their names! Over a decade later, when God called us to Panama City, Panama, my wife and I remember a specific time that we were walking in our neighborhood when we met Keith, a fellow missionary with Wycliffe, and the first words out of his mouth were that he and his wife were just praying for us that morning. That prayer sustained us through some of the most difficult days of planting the new church in a different country. Simply put, the churches we had the opportunity to plant could not have been planted without God's grace and the power of prayer.

Pray, then go

> "And he said to them, 'The harvest is plentiful, but the laborers are few. Therefore pray earnestly to the Lord of the harvest to send out laborers into his harvest. Go your way; behold, I am sending you out as lambs in the midst of wolves.'" (Luke 10:2-3)

Jesus has a clear model for prayer and mission in the Gospels. He instructs his disciples to pray, and then he tells them to go.

Prayer first, but not prayer only. We see in a parallel passage in Matthew that, prior to Jesus making the observation about the harvest, the writer observes, "When he saw the crowds, he had compassion for them, because they were harassed and helpless, like sheep without a shepherd" (Matt. 9:36). Our Lord has commanded us to pray for those who were called to labor in his name, to build up one another in faith, and then work together to bring glory to his name. And all of this is motivated by compassion for the lost, the hurting and the needy.

Another element to this passage is the promise of the harvest. Jesus expressly states that the harvest is in abundance. So, the problem is not the harvest; the problem is the laborers. We must pray for more. And this speaks to one of the arguments against church planting: "Why do we need another church? Don't we have enough already?" The answer is emphatically NO! Obedience to Jesus' call to pray will result in new works of the gospel being sprung up, because the harvest needs laborers, and an abundant harvest needs an abundance of different types of laborers. To reach the world, we need more and different churches to reach more and different demographics of people.

But, the temptation is to rely on our strategies, marketing capacity and our human hard work to accomplish these new works of God, especially in the field of church planting. There are so many things to do, but we must look to Jesus first to show us the how behind the why. The good news is that he has given us clarity on where the real war wages, and it is not in implementing the best church planting system, but rather, "we are not waging war according to the flesh. For the weapons of our warfare are not of the flesh but have divine power to destroy strongholds" (2 Cor. 10:3-4). We must enter into humble, dependent prayer before the Lord before we enter into bold, initiative actions for him; this is how we utilize the weapons of our warfare. In fact, it is helpful to explore how prayer actually accomplishes something meaningful and significant.

Prayer is the work

Every church catalyst, church planter and missionary I know speaks of the importance of prayer, yet it is very hard to sustain a constant and consistent prayer movement in church planting. It just doesn't feel like we are accomplishing a lot while we pray. Actions like sharing the gospel, preaching, working on a Bible study or spending time with people far from God are measurable. But prayer is hard work and a slow process that requires patience. Now, there are times when prayer is so dynamic and we see powerful results by the time we say "amen," but most often we labor in prayer for a long time, waiting on God to break through. This makes it easy to forget that prayer is the work.

Paul Billheimer writes on prayer in his book *Destined for the Throne:*

> "[Prayer] is God's way of giving the church on-the-job training in overcoming the forces hostile to God. This world is a laboratory in which those destined for the throne are learning, by actual practice in the prayer closet, how to overcome Satan and his hierarchy. God designed the program of prayer as an apprenticeship for an eternity of reigning with Christ. Here we are learning how to use the weapons of prayer and faith in overcoming and enforcing Christ's victory so dearly bought."[1]

Our communities where our church planters will minister are places of great spiritual conflict. When we are trained to look with spiritual eyes and dig deep below the surface, we see that there are deep and powerful strongholds in place in every town, state and nation. If we want to see the kingdom of God advance throughout the world (or to the ends of the earth), we are going to need to learn to fight with spiritual weapons. Ephesians 6:12 is clear that "we do not wrestle against flesh and blood, but against the rulers, against the authorities, against the cosmic powers over this present

darkness, against the spiritual forces of evil in the heavenly places."
The enemy will not simply let us walk in, proclaim the gospel and
see lives transformed under its power. If we want to see new and
redemptive faith, the restoration of families, the reconciliation of
neighbors and the renewal of a Spirit-filled church, we must recognize that prayer is the work that breaks these strongholds and
ushers in the power of the gospel.

And when we have an increase in the amount of ministry we
must do, this makes prayer all the more important! E.M. Bounds
describes the prayer habits of Martin Luther in his book on prayer:
"Martin Luther, when once asked what his plans for the following
day were, answered: "Work, work, from early until late. In fact,
I have so much to do that I shall spend the first three hours in
prayer."[2] Our efforts for the kingdom must be rooted in prayer for
the kingdom.

Prayer is one of the most powerful weapons we have in ac-
cessing the authority available in heaven and seeing it unleashed
in our communities. Jesus, through his victory on the cross, has
already won the victory. Through prayer we are merely declaring
this victory over the powers of darkness. Paul writes to the Corinthians, "But thanks be to God, who gives us the victory through
our Lord Jesus Christ. Therefore, my beloved brothers, be stead-
fast, immovable, always abounding in the work of the Lord, knowing that in the Lord your labor is not in vain" (1 Cor. 15:57-58).
The work of Jesus on his earthly ministry was comprised of stead-
fast prayer. Joining in his work in the world requires us to faithfully
pray, laboring in intercession for new churches to be birthed out of
an abundance of new disciples.

Practical advice on prayer for established churches

As you move toward the Lord in faithful obedience through
church planting, there are some key ways you can implement
more focused and centered prayer in your churches:

Engage in regular prayer walks in your church's neighborhood. Prayer walks are an effective way to get you and your congregation to look at your community with spiritual eyes. As you begin to see your neighborhoods as mission fields, it will spark a holy imagination of other neighborhoods who also need Jesus. Praying for your local neighbors is a key way to generate excitement about new works of the gospel in general and church planting in particular.

Schedule and promote quarterly nights of prayer. I have discovered that if we open up a time from 7-11 on a weekend night for people to gather together and intercede with and for one another, the Holy Spirit shows up in a powerful way. Bringing together individual members into corporate prayer strengthens the people of God in their relationship with him and with one another. During these times, pray for the lost in your neighborhood, pray for more churches to be planted and for God to raise up laborers who will go into the farthest reaches of the harvest and bring many lost souls home. This type of fervent, active prayer is the fuel that fans the flame of church planting. There is power in pivotal praying.

Out of those nights of prayer, recruit prayer partners who will pray regularly for you, your church and for the vision of making disciples and multiplying churches through church planting. Give them a list of locations, names of church planters or even your vision to plant a church and have them saturate in prayer. Give updates on how the process of finding a church planter is going. Let them be paving the way long before a church planter is identified. You will find that these will be your greatest champions for church planting in your congregation!

Devote dedicated time in your staff and leadership team meetings to praying for the harvest, the raising up of church planters and the organizational and structural needs to support church planting across your region. This puts your vision in front of your leaders, and your time to devote to prayer shows how serious you take it.

Here are some practical ways that you can pray for church planters and for your church to multiply:

- Personal holiness, integrity and protection from the attacks of the enemy (2 Cor. 10:3-6)
- A deep love for the Lord, the word and the lost (Mk. 12:30, 1 Jn. 2:4-6 & 2 Cor. 4:4-6)
- Emotional, physical, spiritual and financial health for church planters and their families (Prov. 17:22, 1 Cor. 6:19-20, 3 Jn. 1:2 & Phil. 4:19-20)
- Spiritual refreshment and personal renewal during the rigors of ministry (Mk. 1:35 & Isa. 30:15)
- To hear the voice of the Lord for culturally helpful strategies to reach their neighborhoods and communities (Isa. 30:21)
- Open doors to proclaim the gospel clearly and boldly both in personal evangelism and in preaching (Col. 4:3)
- Unity within their church plant launch team, church body and with other churches and ministries (Jn. 17:20-23 & Eph. 4:1-4)
- Strong, clear, servant leadership for their church plant team as they disciple and train church members (Jn. 13:3-4)
- A unified commitment among family members so that the enemy would have no inroads into their homes (Eph. 6:1-4)

Jesus came into the world to save us from our sins. Without him we are completely lost. Now God has given us the ministry of reconciliation. As Paul says in 2 Corinthians 5, we now have the ministry of reconciliation because we have been reconciled back to God. There are so many lost people in our world that need a Savior, and we have been given the opportunity to work alongside of God to bring about his perfect plan. Our part is twofold: pray and then go. As we immerse ourselves in prayer, we see God's kingdom expand and his gospel go to the ends of the earth.

3

Who makes a good church planter?

MARLAN MINCKS

Director of the Converge Church Planting
Assessment Center

If you have not been in a church planting culture, or you are not surrounded by church planters, it can be difficult to wrap your mind around what would make someone be able to take that big step of forming a new family of faith. At first glance, it might seem like there may be no church planter-types around you. Yet, there are more than likely many people in your circle of influence who may be "sleeper" planters just waiting to be activated by the right vision.

2 Peter 1:3 contains a promise that I believe is for the local church: "His divine power has granted to us all things that pertain to life and godliness..." Time and time again, we see the early church being given exactly what they need, when they need it. For instance, when Paul wants to share the gospel and plant churches

in Asia Minor, God restricts him for a time (Acts 16:6). This seems to make no sense in the moment, because he even passed through that region! Why would God not allow him to preach? But we see just a few chapters later that God allows Paul to stay in Ephesus for two years, teaching, training and sending enough missionaries so that "all the residents of Asia heard the word of the Lord" (Acts 19:10). God knew what the church needed to advance, and he granted them everything they needed to advance the gospel in the best way possible.

God has the same plan for your church. Church planting is a good work that will produce new life and godliness among his people, and he will give you what you need to accomplish the calling he has given you. In this chapter, we are going to explore some qualities that would help you spot a good church planter and where you can find them.

How to spot planters

First, look for several behaviors that may help you spot a potential church planter. Behaviors are different than intellectual assent. It is easy to intellectually affirm the statement "we should practice evangelism," but evangelistic behaviors actually tell us if someone lives evangelistically. Evangelistic leaders should know the names of the last person they led to faith in Christ or who they are currently having spiritual conversations with little effort. If you have to think about it, you are not living as if "we should practice evangelism" is true. This speaks to a deeper understanding of belief. What a person DOES proves what they believe, not what they SAY.

Because of this, always look for behaviors over intellectual assent. The question then becomes, what are the behaviors we are looking for in a church planter?

Look for starters

"What have you started" is always a good first question to ask. A church is a difficult thing to get going, even if someone may have started multiple ministries or businesses before. What we don't want is someone's first startup to be a church.

Often, you will find people who have started businesses, ministries, nonprofits or events right in your circle of influence. Start with them, asking questions as to what God might be saying to them about their next steps in life. You might be surprised by what you hear. Look for a demonstrated behavior that points to concrete things they have started, not just someone's intellectual assent that says, "I'd like to try that." Experience counts when it comes to the challenge of building something new from the ground up. Usually, this behavior defines someone as a person. For me, my kids joke that every day of their lives started with hearing me say, "OK, here is what we are going to do!" Starters start things.

Look for gatherers and developers

No one can plant a church alone, that would just be a very private Bible study. God intended for his church to grow amongst other people; there are no solo missions in church planting. Church planters need people, not only to attend but also to help. These people will need to become leaders to lead alongside of the planter, sharing the heavy load of ministry. One of the marks of this type of catalytic leader is that they are natural gatherers. They share a compelling vision that gets other people to get up and get involved, bringing the church's vision to fruition.

This type of person does not just gather, but they also develop others, teaching them how to lead well, and sharing the best of what God has given them to grow others around them. These people don't care who gets the credit. They are not looking for accolades. They are looking for others to be the best disciples and leaders they can be.

The reality is that those who make good disciples and good leaders were discipled and led well. Does this person have a discipleship background? Do they naturally see where they are leading others? Can they share what the finished product looks like? These types of disciplers and leaders often have a plan for developing people from new believers to fully committed followers of Christ who will make disciples. They have a plan that goes beyond a service on Sundays. Leaders lead things and disciplers disciple.

Look for family men

The toughest thing anyone can do is walk into the enemy's territory and start a life-giving, transformational church. Satan's easiest target to stop a church planter is his family. He targeted Job's family to prove that Job only followed God for the benefits he would receive. What makes us think that Satan would not attack a church planter where it will hurt the most? A church planter who puts his family second is a church planter who won't last.

Good disciple-makers and leaders are the ones who know how to disciple and lead those closest to them. Demonstrated experience and success in this area is paramount for selecting the right planter. Here are some questions to ask of someone you are considering:

- What is your intentional plan to disciple your wife and family, and how is that going?
- Do you have clear family and ministry boundaries?
- Do you spend quality time with your children? When was the last time and what did that look like?
- Do you still date your wife? When was the last time you went on a date?
- Would your family say that they are put first? What behaviors do you practice to demonstrate they are first priority?

Leaders and disciplers who are the "real deal" will lead and disciple their family.

Look for doers

Those who do the work of ministry know the labor and the heartbreak of serving. It takes a toll on even the most experienced pastor — the emotional investment itself seems to be endless. And when it comes to church planting, the lack of structure and resources makes the work 10,000 times harder. Planters put a massive amount of time in on a seemingly never-ending list of to-do's and often with no help and little money. Because of this, consistent and faithful performance under pressure is a critical behavioral trait to look for in a candidate.

What has their past work experience shown? Were they good employees? Did they get good references? In my role as the director of the Church Planting Assessment Center for Converge, I have actually seen where someone's mother said in a reference, "Don't let them plant. They won't follow through."

Church planters must be able to grind it out in the toughest days, and those are the majority of days in ministry. You cannot teach grit, but you can utilize it immensely over time. Doers keep the ministry of church planting going.

Look for flexible planners

While planters need to have a plan and a vision and be able to bring that to fruition, they also need to be flexible. Things change, especially in light of limited structure, systems and resources. It seems like things shift exponentially in a church planting context. Seldom have I heard any planter say that the church turned out exactly as he had envisioned it. Flexibility is an undervalued strength that comes with time and experience. Someone who has been in ministry or leadership must be able to, in the famous Marine slogan, "adapt and overcome." Those who highly value structure and cannot handle deviation from a plan might not be the best fit in a church planting context.

And yet, there is also a need to ensure flexibility is balanced with the ability to plan and execute a strategy. Planters must be sure of their calling, and willing to commit to a strategy with enough confidence to withstand external pressures to change. A weak leader (or someone trying to "wing it") can be easily overrun by people who have the wrong intentions and every church has those who show up looking for power. It takes strength and resolve to stand up against those people with a solid, well thought-out plan that is flexible enough to change.

This balance of flexibility and planning can be a difficult one to assess, and there is never going to be a perfect church planter, but having these key skills can be an indicator of a potentially successful leader to invest in.

Where to find planters

Now that we have highlighted some of the behaviors of a potential church planter, the next question is: Where to look? As we stated at the beginning of this chapter, sometimes these dynamic leader are hiding in plain sight, especially in established churches that might not have had the eye for the type of leaders it takes to plant. Knowing a few places where there might be "sleeper" planters could give you a huge advantage when looking for more avenues to advance the gospel through planting.

In your congregation

Often, the hardest people to see potential lying in wait are those closest to you. Familiarity can make extraordinary gifts seem commonplace. But what do others say about key leaders in your church? Are there leaders that people in your church go to in a time of crisis? Do these leaders consistently have others coming to them to assist in solving problems? If the answer is yes, you might have a "sleeper" planter in your midst.

Seeing how others treat a potential planter will help you not to rely solely on your own judgement. God's church has a knack for confirming godly and gifted people, and there are additional ways to investigate someone's potential by giving him leadership and seeing how the church responds. Connecting someone with a high level of potential with other pastors who have planted is another great way to get a read on his capacity and gifts.

I used to pheasant hunt with an ex-Marine friend. That guy could spot a feather or a beak of a bird a hundred yards off the road. For every bird I would see, he had spotted 50. I asked him one day, "How do you see so many more birds than me?" He replied, "I guess I just know what I'm looking for." The truth is, most of us don't know what we are looking for, so rely on the church and others who have planted to help you spot potential. You might be surprised what you find.

In youth ministry

Some of the best church planters we have seen over the years were at one time youth pastors. It takes unmeasurable amounts of energy and innovation to plant a church, and these just so happen to be some of the same skills it takes to sustain a vibrant youth ministry. Also, considering how church plants tend to be reaching those who are in the upcoming generation in their beginning years, church planters coming out of a next-gen ministry context are already equipped to know how to reach the demographic most likely to join a young church. And since youth pastors tend to fall just short on the scale of ADD, they make some of the best people to do the unthinkable and risk everything to start a new church to reach those who are unreached.

A potential planter coming from this context will also already have demonstratable ministry skills, observable behavioral patterns and reproduceable systems to adapt to a church planting context. Look around your area for youth pastors who may need someone to ask them the question, "Have you ever thought about planting a church?"

In associate pastors

Many associate pastors have a wealth of experience with

church and ministry. For associates to be successful, they have to be able to build systems and structures in which people thrive, but also where they can relate and connect with others. They are skilled at implementing vision, seeing what works and what doesn't. If they are wired to plant, they can be great at starting a new church and take the systems and structures they have developed and adapt them to a new context. They also often have deep ministry connections in established local churches that can help fund and resource a new church startup.

For some, they have been waiting for their chance to lead from the first chair. For others, they enjoy leading from the second chair, but have unknown and untapped skills of vision and pioneering. Not all successful associate pastors have the skills for a lead planter role, but many do and are underutilized in their ministry. All it takes is a simple ask!

In the marketplace

If you are interested in finding planters, you can sharpen your eye and see them everywhere. I recall a church planter from Wisconsin who was a veterinarian. It turns out that God was calling him to start a new church and many of his customers (the farmers, not the animals!) he served turned out to be crucial partners with him in that new gospel work. He was in a local barn!

Those who are most skilled at connecting with nonbelievers and those who are disconnected from church are often…wait for it… working outside of the church! So as you look at godly businessmen and skilled leaders working in professional businesses, they might be "sleeper" planters simply waiting for the right vision and the right time to make the step into full-time ministry work. Remember, you don't need a degree to plant a church or lead in ministry, but you need a love for Jesus and a clear call to serve his church.

In church planting contexts

The 21st century has seen an increased emphasis on church

planting in North America. Even in the mid-1990s, there were precious few books on church planting, and it was certainly not something that was celebrated or even perceived to be effective in a broad sense. But now there are leaders, movements, books and conferences on church planting that are of great value. Take advantage of this trend and the popularity with which people are drawn to these larger events.

Go to these conferences with the express purpose of meeting potential planters; this is the place where many will choose to go to dip their feet into the church planting waters. At these conferences there are also ample opportunities to speak with church planting groups. Offer to host a network event at your church one Sunday. Ask for conferences to be held in your area to help bring church planters in and encourage them in their journey. And above all, keep an open hand and a prayerful heart to see how going to these events can be used by God to bring more church planters into your midst.

Bring it together

Being a church planter is a complex and nuanced calling. A person has to be a starter, developer, leader, communicator and pastor while working under less-than-ideal conditions. It's not for everybody and it's certainly not for the faint of heart. Determining who might be a good fit is also complicated and not always entirely clear. You might have a seasoned and skilled leader, but he does not have the necessary self-starter, entrepreneurial skills to develop and lead a team from scratch. But you might have someone who has been in the wings and on the fringe, quietly serving in the background, who is just waiting for the right vision and the right person to communicate God's call in just the right way, and he could be our most successful planter yet. So how do we know?

The good news is, you're not alone. We can take these behavior traits and locations, and do our best to be on the lookout. But there is also a wealth of church planting resources available to you, especially assessment centers, that can be a significant mile marker on the road to planting. Converge has a tried and true assessment process that has been honed from over 30 years of experience and best practices. We use a 16 building-block grid that potential planters are assessed against to determine if they are wired to plant and what they will need to do to prepare for it. This is a major reason why our church planting success rates are so high; we know how to vet the right people for this specialized ministry. And you can be a part of it too! Many pastors see things differently after taking part in this assessment.

We need local church pastors to catch this vision for church planting and be our boots on the ground. We must find and wake our "sleeper" planters who are among us to continue advancing the gospel through new works and new plants that will reach new demographics of people who desperately need to hear the message of Jesus.

4

Recruiting and developing church planters

ED MARCELLE

Lead Pastor of Terra Nova Church in Troy, New York,
and Senior Pastor of the Terra Nova Network

Throughout the Bible, God consistently prepares the people he calls. It seems almost a given that those tasked with doing great things for God are the ones who experience pain, conflict and a period of development. Moses spent 40 years in Pharaoh's court and another 40 herding sheep in preparation for leading Israel. John the Baptist spent almost 30 years in the wilderness to prepare for only six months of ministry. Jesus himself was a carpenter for 30 years for only three years of public ministry before his death, resurrection and ascension. Time and time again, we see God values who we are becoming more than what we do for him, and that is shown by his emphasis on preparation and development.

Church planting is a great work for the kingdom, and the

most successful planters are the ones who have come out of an established church and went through a season of development and training. In the previous chapter, we discussed how to identify church planters; now we must address how to recruit and then develop them well. To this end, I have used the acronym SPAN — surface, prepare, activate and network — as I work with would-be church planters.

All four of these areas represent their own challenges. Surfacing and recruiting a church planting pastor is a challenging and crucial part of successfully planting churches that requires much patience, prayer and faith-filled action. This necessitates creating an intersection of opportunity and interest that may help a future church leader find his calling and then follow you as you walk with him through it.

Preparing a planter is a balancing act. Do we prepare too much in terms of study and produce leaders who can pass theological tests but are poor disciples? Do we send out families who are ill-prepared for the realities of life in full-time ministry and therefore run the risk of devastating failure?

In large part, with careful planning and genuine care for people, we can reduce the risks inherent in each of these areas. Specifically, in terms of preparing church planters, Converge's assessment center has been successful in figuring out how to balance theological knowledge with a focus on personal discipleship. Activating or launching a planter will require overcoming or avoiding bureaucratic, financial and personnel pitfalls that can stall or destroy a church plant. And finally, networking with other churches requires a planter to speak to multiple cultural languages and respect differences in nonessentials. Small issues, whether perceived or historical, can disrupt relationships among churches and denominations and could prevent financial or relational backing.

The two most crucial areas when considering established church pastors is related to recruitment and development of church planters. Especially when a church has both a desire and resources to devote toward planting, it is vital to know how to bring a planter along on your team and then place him through a period of training and preparation to be set up well to plant a strong and healthy church. This chapter will address these two major elements.

Recruiting church planters

Once you know some of the keys on how to spot church planters, the next step is to find out how to recruit them and create an environment for these future leaders to thrive in your established church context. Many planters have a restlessness that can cause them to be excited to plant, but often negative toward established churches that "do it the way they've always done it." Part of your role can be to help bring a redemptive and helpful view of a mature, local church that can advance the mission of God toward the front lines of church planting. Recruiting potential planters to come into your context for training and preparation is a key part of being involved in church planting, and a helpful church will recruit church planters with more than money, but with culture, collaboration, communication and celebration.

Shape a culture of church planting

Have you ever told your congregation about an upcoming event, used multiple vehicles of communication (like social media, Sunday morning slides and announcements) and yet had more than one person come to you and say, "I had no idea this event was even happening"? Most pastors have had this infuriating experience more often than we'd like to admit. It seems like people don't hear us, don't remember what we say or misunderstand what we are trying to get done.

As frustrating as this typical scenario is, it teaches us a lesson. The reality stands that we need to speak more clearly to our churches. And when we are trying to recruit church planters, we need to communicate our passion about this more frequently, in more platforms and with greater clarity until other people know your vision and say it as well as you do.

If you are forming a church planting passion in your church, talk about it often! Speak about the whys of church planting, the need for church planting and your church's potential role in church planting regularly. Call people to church planting from the pulpit and in your small groups or classes. Let your congregation know you are praying for church leaders to be surfaced from your congregation, and that you are keeping an eye out on how to spot church planters and you are intentionally going to places to find them. This level of communication and culture takes a long time to develop, but it will be worth it in the long run. It creates a "normal" environment for a church planter to walk into. If you communicate often and clearly enough about church planting, your people will not be surprised when church planters show up! You can incubate an environment over time that is conducive to recruiting church planters.

Collaborate with existing church plants, churches and planting organizations

Sometimes a plant is being planned in your city, and you may not even know about it. Many churches have a "ground warfare" strategy when it comes to beginning a church. Meeting people in coffee shops, local art galleries and going to non-church events and meeting unchurched people are the norm. So, if they are not running in the circles you are running in, you could potentially have a church plant right near you and not know about it. Look at local papers, join local church planting groups on Facebook and keep an eye out for denominations and networks that have a presence in your area. God might be saving you a lot of effort by bringing someone right to your front door!

Because of this it is always good for the churches in an area to communicate regularly with one another. Meeting with other pastors regularly will offer the best chance to plant a healthy church and become aware of what is going on in your city. This collaboration can have some great kingdom impact. For instance, a church may have funds but no leader for a plant. Another church may have pioneer families in an area eager to launch a new congregation but no funding. A third church may have a leader who is excited to plant a church, but they don't have as many families willing to be a part of that plant, or the money to fully support the planter. Keeping communication open with other churches in your area will allow you to work with other pastors in collaborative ministries when possible.

Also, church planting organizations work across large regions and often have church planting specialists who can connect you with potential planters looking for a home church. Check with regional and national bodies to see if they have leads in your area and volunteer to follow up with them. Many groups work with other denominations and groups.

Communicate with church planters winsomely

When you find a potential planter and want to recruit him to partner with you, let it be known from the very beginning that you have a passion and desire to help plant churches, and that the planter in front of you could be an answer to your prayer for more kingdom works. Often planters feel competitive "vibes" from established church pastors, or that they will be a token that a church can put forward and say "see, we plant churches too" without actually coming alongside and meaningfully contributing. Some church plants have even been railroaded by established church pastors who want to control and manipulate rather than come alongside and support. When you show yourself as an ally in the cause of Christ, you will be helpful and much more successful in recruiting planters to join you.

Ask the planter about his vision, and see if that vision aligns with your church planting goals. Be up front, share what resources you may be able to offer, and how this planter would be able to help you in your ministry goals to support church planting. The goal for connecting is to see if your visions can align together and you can partner together. A word of caution here: You don't want or need exact alignment of ministry philosophy or goals, but rather you're looking for the ability and willingness to partner together to send the planter out. Of course, there are certain non-negotiables, but when you give clear metrics and parameters, often differing philosophies can partner together and contribute to one another to successfully plant churches. The goal is the gospel and the kingdom, not replicating the same culture or the same exact church methodology. Having this approach is winsome, and can greatly help you recruit church planters to join your team to be sent out from your established church context.

Celebrate church planting

The things we celebrate are the things to which our congregations will gravitate. In order to create a church planting culture and an environment for recruiting planters, you need to celebrate church planting. Using your social media to promote church plants and planters is one way to start this. As you let your congregation know what plants you support, you shape a welcoming environment for church planters.

Another way to celebrate is to invite planters in to talk about their ministries. This has been the single most effective way our church has engaged our congregation in promoting an understanding of and passion for church planting. As you put forward and endorse other church planters to share their vision in your context, you can use that to leverage your vision and also promote collaboration, unity and celebrate the work of God through church planting. When the conversation moves from the theoretical to the practical with a church planter on stage talking, that's when the rubber hits the road with vision.

Developing church planters

The church we planted, Terra Nova, has planted two churches out of our mother church in the last six years. Both required the usual pieces to be in place: The elders were behind the plan, we had people from those areas who would form a core, and we had set aside funds for the plant. The leaders for each of these plants — Terra Nova in Saratoga Springs, New York, and Terra Nova in North Adams, Massachusetts — both came from within the mother church in Troy, New York.

The two leaders are very different men who had dramatically divergent paths that led to planting from amongst our context. One had gone to Bible college and was in seminary, had wanted to go into ministry and became an intern. The other was a high-level finance executive with a wide-open career path, no formal Bible training and originally had no desire or calling to be a pastor prior to becoming heavily involved in ministry at Terra Nova. As we have discussed in the previous chapter, often the future leaders of our churches are in our midst, just waiting to be activated.

So how do we help people from varied backgrounds realize and develop toward their calling? What structures allow you to create this pipeline of leaders in the life of your church? The following systems can help create the structural dynamics for leadership development in the local church.

Create shared spaces for potential leaders

When Jesus trained his disciples, he brought them along to see ministry, shared ministry life with them and coached their strengths and weaknesses before sending them out. He did not ask them to "ready, fire, aim," but rather there was a built-in healthy exposure to ministry prior to the disciples being sent. "Follow me" was the first command of Jesus' ministry and training philosophy.

With this in mind, giving planters invitations to "follow you" in shared ministry is important. Only those who have spent time serving the local church should be sent out to start a church, so it is key to create places where potential planters can serve practical needs in your church alongside you or other mature leaders. This will highlight their strengths, areas of growth and even potential pitfalls that you can coach them to avoid. It is a genuinely powerful encouragement when I tell people that we have been praying about a ministry and have been praying about a person for it, and we all think it is you. Give them the space to make mistakes. Let them learn and live to do another ministry. Operating with a shared space where it is safe to fail is essential to develop leaders to rise to the occasion when there is more at stake. I certainly got that opportunity and am grateful for it.

Leadership Collective

The Leadership Collective was a program I started to train potential ministry leaders at Terra Nova Church. Men and women in whom we noticed a ministry presence and desire, a theological spark or a devotion of their personal life were invited. This was also a place to invite planters who we had recruited. Over the course of a year, we would read books and articles together, and then gather frequently to share a devotional (led by a participant) and discuss what we were learning.

It gave three great things to our people who were being developed as ministry leaders and planters. First, they were recognized for their service. People took it as an honor to have the church leadership recognize and invite them into this collective. We helped make a big deal of that in having a dinner at a local brew pub where I could thank them, challenge them and give an orientation to the program. Second, they were given resources and time that helped build them for future ministry and planting. Third, they were part of a group of peer leaders that allowed for an "iron sharpening iron." Good things happen when you create connections among your church's key influencers and those pursuing planting. Those meetings reaped a great benefit for our church and put some people on the road to full-time ministry, including multiple church planters.

Our former banker turned church planter in North Adams, Massachusetts, excelled in this setting. He wanted to serve the church and was eager to read theology and discuss it. His time in the Leadership Collective also demonstrated that he was teachable, faithful and growing in his walk with the Lord. He and his wife were great small group leaders and people were growing under that ministry. When he had the opportunity to preach, I realized we had a church leader in our midst who was already being developed and prepared!

Internships

Another opportunity we created at Terra Nova Church was a program where young people who were interested in vocational ministry (including people that could potentially be planters) were exposed to different areas of service within our church. This is where the pastor of our Saratoga Springs plant started. The internship always starts with an intake conversation with a pastor. This young man started out thinking he would teach at a Bible college because he wanted to teach the Bible to change lives. But over time, he learned that the local church offered this and so much more. In his time at the internship, we shared books, went out to lunch to discuss ministry and put up some money for his online seminary bill. As we did this, he developed a more focused call to plant. His internship meant broad exposure to various ministries, room for discussion and time with other pastors, and a plan at the end for further development and service.

Residency

Our Terra Nova Network also launched a residency program. The difference between an internship and a residency is this: The internship seeks to expose an interested person to various ministries to help identify a call; the residency takes a committed person and exposes them to the inner workings of the church, the ministry of church planting and (for us) the culture of the Northeast mission field.

Over a two-year period, the resident is taught the church culture and tools, handed a ministry to start and lead to fruition, given a budget and direction for conferences and classes, and given constant feedback from a mentoring pastor. Finally, the resident creates his proposal for planting and is assisted with networking and fundraising before planting.

The value of patience and prayer

Recruiting and developing church planters raises many questions given the specifics of the situation. Many church planters simply want a friend and a place to grow, develop and prepare to plant. Good planters recognize the need for development and an established church context to plant out of. But some need to be encouraged to see how you can come alongside them. Honesty of communication, a culture built to accept church planters, collaboration with others and continual celebration of church planting will help you recruit planters into your midst.

Some things to consider in development are calling (are they confident they want to plant?), experience (how much exposure do they have to ministry?), place (where do they want to plant?) and developmental needs (where do they need to be developed?). Answering these questions will help you know where and how to place them in development in your church.

These things will take patience. It took three years for us to see the leader of our first plant recruited, trained and sent out. It will take prayer. The church and planter need to be reliant on the Lord for leading. It will take bold churches ready to face the impossible, ready to risk vision and give their lives to their church and the church of the future.

The Lord will build his church. He has leaders for us. He will care for his church. The challenging, sometimes terrifying and often satisfying part is that he wants to use us in this process of recruiting and developing leaders for the next church!

Being the church a church planter needs

LEE STEPHENSON

Lead Pastor of Harvest Community Church
& Executive Director of Church Planting, Converge

Have you ever had someone try to help you, but he or she ended up making a mess of things? I can remember when one of my friends told me his kids tried to make breakfast for his wife on Mother's Day. The concoction was a strange mixture of cereal, oatmeal, milk and orange juice. It was a beautiful gesture of love, but not very practical or helpful. In fact, it caused a big mess! For many churches seeking to plant, a similar experience can happen. Without the right understanding of what a church planter needs, a well-meaning sending church can be more of a hassle than a help. As we explore this more in-depth, it is important to remember that qualified church planters are strong in their faith and value the local church to such a degree they want to start one. Not only is the church near and dear to their hearts, but they don't want to take this gigantic leap of faith without an established church behind them. They want to collaborate, and they need your help in key areas for them to succeed. Some experienced planters recognize their need for collaboration, and some do not know yet how much they need you. Well-trained planters have a deeply rooted passion to work together and leverage multiple ministries to see the gospel come to bear in a new community among a new people, and those who are less experienced need to see the value an established church can provide.

Many church planters feel alienated and lost as they feel the church (and sometimes their church) has given up on them. Some established churches feel threatened by the very skills it takes to plant a new work. Also, it is easy to look around and see churches with incredible resources for kingdom expansion, yet no desire to assist in church planting. The last thing they want is to be abandoned as they walk by faith out to the frontlines of discipleship and evangelism.

In this chapter, we address several ways that an established church can be the "wind in the sails" for a church planter. However, the power is generated not through the eyes of the parent church but begins when you place yourself in the shoes of the church planter. In other words, what is it that church planters are looking for? What do they need? And what are they asking for? It is vital that a sending church knows how to come alongside a planter and be the church a church planter needs.

Encouragement

Do you remember the feeling of being lost as a child? Maybe in the grocery store or at a public event, and the feeling of turning around and not seeing an adult you know and trust nearby?

I know from firsthand experience that feeling in the pit of your stomach is the same whether you're a child or an adult. Rushing around trying to find something of familiarity and praying to see a person you know or recognize comes with the experience of being lost. What's interesting is that the fears of loneliness and insecurity intensify the longer you are on your own. This pit-of-your-stomach reality is what many church planters feel as they leave the comfort of an established church to follow the call of God on their life.

And the more pioneering the church plant process is the lonelier the endeavor can be for the planter. Ministry is difficult enough as it is, but multiply that feeling by 1000 times and that is the loneliness many planters feel starting a new church. One of the primary things that a parent church needs to offer a church planter and his family is encouragement.

An established church needs to find ways to encourage a church planter and his family on a consistent basis, especially as they process the intense joys and pains of planting. This happens when the established church sees its ministry to church planters as an extension of its overall ministry and not as a distraction or hindrance to the overall effectiveness of the church. Consider some of the following ideas for encouraging and connecting with church planters:

- Encourage church staff and attendees to have a meal or coffee with the church planter or the planter's family on a regular schedule.
- Bless the church planting family with gift cards to local restaurants or to the movies. Some of the most meaningful gifts my wife and I received were gifts that were given directly to my kids with the note to do something special for their parents. This engaged my kids and gave them a positive view of ministry and the church.
- Allow the church planter to preach for you and/or have a significant role from time to time with the congregation.
- Recruit a few families to "adopt" the church planter's family as a personal ministry.

The best ways to be an encouragement is to be consistent and intentional. A church planter does not need a list of what they are doing wrong; they need a trusted, established church and friends who will encourage them in the midst of the challenge of ministry. An established church has the continuity and people to create a balanced and healthy framework of encouragement for a church planter and his family.

Comfort and sympathy

To be entirely honest, one of the reasons I got into church planting was to avoid the existing conflicts of an already established church. In my thinking, established churches were made up of established people who were filled with pre-existing conflicts and I thought I would avoid all of this through planting a new work. I was 100% wrong! I found church planting to be filled with unique and nuanced conflicts and relational struggles. The only difference was that these problems were created under my watch, and that was a tough pill to swallow.

That reality, in and of itself, demands the need for a sending church to be compassionate, kind and gentle with its church planters. Often they feel guilt for the problems in their church, thinking, "If I only did this better then things would be different." Offering comfort in crisis, and sympathy in all times and with all matters, is invaluable for the hard-hitting, self-starting planter who needs a safe place to be vulnerable and heal.

What I eventually learned was that challenge, crisis and conflict simply reside in all spiritual ministry. Any time people join together to accomplish a goal, these things are going to be present. And I have experienced firsthand that in the first three years of a plant almost every church planter is going to face three major challenges/crises: financial, personal and leadership.

One of the key vulnerabilities of any family is their finances. We need money to survive in our world. And whether it be an unexpected tax bill, loss of personal missionary support, increased overhead without enough tithing to support it or a wealth of other issues, the devil will exploit any opportunity to thwart the work of a church planter and his team. Church planting is spiritual warfare. Any time a planter steps out of the fold and declares new territory for the kingdom of God, all hell breaks loose trying to rob and destroy this work from ever happening. Financial difficulties cause immense strain on a family, and I have seen church planters taken out of the playing field because the financial strain was too much. Many times this type of attack is rooted in distracting from the work of the ministry.

It is also not uncommon for planters to face a personal physical and/or emotional hardship while planting. This is present even in my own story with both of our church plants. In the first, I went through a series of five surgeries in 20 months; one of those left me bedridden for almost 12 weeks and preaching from a wheelchair for two months. In my second plant, a month after our grand opening I had a total knee replacement at the age of 39. Not only were the physical challenges incredibly demanding and stressful, they created emotional heartache too. Discouragement and fear are always tools in Satan's arsenal, and attacking the physical or emotional state of a church planter and his family is always a "go-to" strategy.

A church planter will also likely face a unique and nuanced leadership challenge during the first three years. If people aren't following their shepherd, they're lost. And if they lose confidence in their shepherd, they will wander. This is another way the devil will seek to divide and conquer a new work of the gospel. At about the 2½-year period in our church plant, I was recovering from a major knee surgery and an elder became publically vocal against me and my leadership. There was pressure to change how we were being led, and this person wanted more voice and influence and was willing to stir up questions about me in order to get it. I was out recovering and relearning to walk, obviously away from the church, but was gifted by God with a solid elder board and a team of wise counselors who challenged him on his issues, fought for unity and kept me informed while I was healing. This person ultimately left the church and we moved forward, but it was an incredibly difficult season for us.

Understanding and expecting these challenges is important for any parent church as it sends someone to plant. Now, these things already exist in the life of established churches, but most established churches have leaders and systems in place to help in these moments of challenge and crisis. Church planters are often new, leading from the front where they don't have the systems, structures or support to soften the blows. Every challenge hits a planter square on the jaw. Parent churches need to be sympathetic to what the team is experiencing and find ways to comfort them in the midst of it. Here are some practical thoughts as to how a church can show sympathy and comfort:

- Create a prayer team that stays in touch with the planters/leaders and commits to weekly praying for the family needs.
- Create space for both lead pastors to connect regularly over coffee. (Tip: Keep it more relational than making it a coaching relationship.)
- Practically support the church plant by sending people to stop in and attend/serve on a Sunday.
- Create the avenue for the planter to feel that the parent church leadership is safe.

Encouragement must be sympathetic and carry the comfort of a shepherd. When you leave a meeting with a church planter, you want them to be supported and assured he is not alone in this journey.

Fellowship

In my experience, I found that church planting creates opportunities for crisis. This means that church planting can be one of the most discouraging and frustrating works in ministry, but it can also be the crucible for change and the development of character unlike any other environment. Church planters can turn a crisis into growth if they have good fellowship with a pastor who will consistently motivate them to go to Jesus with their pain, receive his grace and then mature through the crisis. You cannot have this level of spiritual direction without consistent fellowship and the trust that sprouts up through it.

Paul writes to the church in Philippi and asks them to "complete my joy by being of the same mind, having the same love, being in full accord and of one mind." (Phil. 2:2). The word that can be used to describe what Paul was referencing is the word *fellowship*. Fellowship is rooted in relationship, not in an activity or program. The common ground that allows fellowship to take place is a shared sense of partnership centered on faith in Jesus Christ. True fellowship is something that doesn't naturally just happen, but has to be fostered intentionally over time.

Church planters are naturally independent. They like venturing into the unknown, enjoying and even taking pride in living life with a self-reliant attitude. The strength of this mentality is they walk by faith into the unknown, but shadow to this is a fierce pride that doesn't ask for help when necessary. Additionally, it is easy for a parent church to enable self-destructive independence by simply forgetting about the needs of a church plant. Often the phrase "out of sight…out of mind" rings with an established church unless intentional structures are put in place to prevent that from happening. This forgetfulness often creates a relational gap between the sending church and its church plant.

The solution to burnout and something that an established church pastor can provide is proximity. Proximity breeds trust. Proximity and trust over time breeds intimacy. And this fellowship provides a support structure that is one of the biggest blind spots yet one of the most impactful things for a church planter.

The key to keeping fellowship is to recognize that different philosophies and methodologies should never get in the way of this fellowship. Of course, a church planter will do things differently — that's why he's planting! But the intentional fostering of an ongoing fellowship between established and new churches can be a huge gift to both. Having a place where the planter feels connected and known in the early days gives a naturally independently minded leader a place to feel connected until this new work gets more relationally established. Over time, fellowship between churches will look differently, but especially in the beginning it will be well worth the time investment. Here are some ways to develop fellowship between a parent and daughter church:

- In the first couple of years, look for ways to spend time together.
- Plan a few times a year to invite the planter and leadership team to staff meetings, trainings or celebrations.
- Invite the church planter to make a video or come and share updates with the church from time to time.
- Teach the church to talk positively about the other church as much as they can in the community.
- Offer to serve on the board until the plant has time to develop internal leadership.

Being the church a church planter needs

Regardless of experience, age or methodological gaps, a church planter needs to be in relationship to and remembered by his parent church. As an already established church, look for opportunities to encourage, comfort, sympathize and spend time together. Most likely you have invested time, resources and people in getting this new work off the ground, but once it's started that's when the real relational element comes into play. Even as they grow more independent, planters still need to know you are there and that they matter to you.

Recognizing the pitfalls of entrepreneurial leadership and the difficulties of church planting can go a long way in allowing an established church's leadership to empathize with the extreme stress and struggle of a new gospel work. This requires laying aside what YOU think they need, and truly seek to serve your church plant in humility, as Jesus continually serves his church. An established church can truly be the "wind in the sails" of starting a church that has potential to reach an entirely new group of people, if your wind is blowing in the right direction. We need churches to come alongside for the long haul, and truly be the church a church planter needs.

6

Funding the vision of church planting

DANNY PARMELEE

Vice President of Church Planting,
Converge MidAmerica

"Where will we get the money and the people?" is a common question and hang-up for potential church planting churches. I have seen a number of churches that never take that brave first step because they are intimidated by the perceived financial cost. And yes, it is true that a church plant does require many financial resources to start, but there are ways to participate and mitigate that financial impact to make it possible and achievable for every church to play a role in planting.

The first step is recognizing that you alone are not responsible to provide all the resources for a church plant. Here is what Paul says about money to the Corinthians:

"Each one must give as he has decided in his heart, not reluctantly or under compulsion, for God loves a cheerful giver. And God is able to make all grace abound to you, so that having all sufficiency in all things at all times, you may abound in every good work." (2 Cor. 9:7-8)

Many pastors know this first verse and reference it often, but few remember the second. Our church planting efforts, especially when we consider how to financially partner, should come out of a place of God-centric worship, cheerful willingness and genuinely winsome faith. Yet the second verse is so powerful. It is God who is able to make grace abound. It is God who is sufficient in all things at all times. And it is God's equipping and grace that allows us to abound in every good work. Church planting is a good work for God's kingdom, and it is ultimately his responsibility to raise the funds for it to happen. Coupled with our prayer, obedience and faith, he can raise however much money his church needs to thrive. We must begin with this basic element of faith and confidence in the power of God to raise the funds for his work.

It is also important to remember that church planters know they will have to raise a substantial amount of their own funding to cover salary and initial operational expenses. It is their calling, and their faithful partnership with the work of the Holy Spirit will ultimately raise the funds necessary and confirm God's will for them to plant a church. I have even seen how God uses a delay in financing to prepare a leader or bring just the right person on the team. Perceived setbacks in fundraising might be the very thing God is using to start his church at just the right time.

With this in mind, a sending or parent church can be a significant partner in this journey. In fact, you can kick-start the engine of support raising in such a way as to heavily impact the outcome! Here are some crucial points to consider as you come alongside church planters and kick-start their fundraising efforts:

Add church planting to your budget

Most churches have a missions budget. But, depending on the criteria that the missions committee has set up, these funds may or may not be available to church planters. For example, some missions committees see serving overseas as the qualifying criteria to receive missions funding from the church. If this is the case, then revisit how domestic church planters can potentially qualify to receive missions funding by adding in a specific line item in the church's budget.

"Follow the money, honey!" Whatever you church truly values, it will spend money on. Creating a line item specifically for church planting support in your budget ensures that your budget reflects a serious and intentional engagement while additionally helping to plan ahead by setting an actual amount. For example, setting your budget to give $100, $500 or $1,000 each month toward church planting creates a need and an expectation to be filled. Make the decision ahead of time whether those finances will go toward a single church planter or multiple. There might be a desire to have a deeper investment in one planter or spread it out to give smaller amounts to a few different plants for broader impact. This depends on the size of your church, the size of your budget and your unique experience and vision for church planting. For instance, if you have raised up a planter from within, you might want to have a deeper and more significant financial impact in one plant. But, if you want to begin a general awareness and spark passion for planting among your congregation, multiple planters that give quarterly updates might be the way to go. Remember that money is an excuse for an ongoing relationship, regardless of your church's size or budget.

No matter which approach you take, the key is to plan ahead and have clear criteria for determining support for church planters. Creating a unique line item in your budget adds priority, expectation and intentional engagement.

Create a church planting savings account

Many churches have special gifts and unique one-time dona-
tions come in at the end of the year. Often, that money is used to
cover gaps in the budget planning, but consider creating a special
savings account designated for planting as a financial commitment
to this important work regardless of what stage in the parenting
process your church finds itself. This could also be used as a place-
holder for designated money in a specific line item that was not
used in the previous fiscal year.

Creating an actual account and not just "keeping it in the
back of your mind" ensures it becomes an area of importance
and focus, especially as that money increases over time. This works
especially well if there is a plan to invest more heavily in a single
plant or if your church is praying for a plant in a specific community nearby. Asking God to raise up a planter and having an
expectant faith to save toward that plant is a great way to model
the character of a church that a church planter can significantly
partner with.

Keep in mind even though there may be a large accumulated
amount that does not mean your church has to give it to the planter all at once. You may still want to distribute funding to a planter
on a monthly installment or in larger gifts as he reaches specific
benchmarks. The important point is the faith to save, regardless
of where you are in the planting process, will do more for your
church and for you than you can imagine.

Partner with local or network churches to create an impact fund

Churches work better when they are working together. Often,
there can be a group of churches that pool their resources to create larger impact over a region. This can be especially effective if
a group of smaller churches contributed just $50-$100 a month
for a church planter. Over a three-year period that could amount
to over $20,000 toward church planting, which could generate a

greater impact and legacy. Partnering together does not necessitate that all the churches contribute an equal amount either.

I was part of a group where some churches contributed $50 a month and others contributed significantly more to a fund that helped many church planters. We had a simple and clear process for who would qualify to receive those funds, how it was determined and how that money was ultimately disbursed. When we made decisions together on who to fund, it allowed every church to feel like an equal contributor to the planter as it was funneled through a shared group account. Pooling resources with clear expectations and processes created much more impact over the long haul. It also created an added benefit of deepening our partnerships together. Collaborating together builds trust and kingdom-centric ministry instead of church-centric ministry.

Give your space away for free

Sometimes, helping in the planter's financial needs isn't directly giving finances but relieving some of the residual costs that come with planting a new work without any inherited resources. Space is always a major cost that eats up a church planter's budget, and giving away or designating some space in your building can be a major help as you are supporting a local plant.

This can be as simple as allowing a daughter church to hold launch team meetings in your boardroom or basement. It could also be giving the church planter a desk and office space to meet, pray and prepare. If you have a larger campus or unused space, you could let them use your sanctuary, basement, chapel or youth area to host services. Sometimes, church plants are willing to meet at off times like Sunday afternoons or Sunday nights, so don't discount creatively using the space God has already provided to advance a new church.

Lend or give away equipment

If your church has been around for years, you may have a collection of equipment that isn't being used. As churches move from building to building or expand, many pastors want to hang onto stuff because they think "someday we might use it." That "someday" is the day you have a church planter walk into your office! Often, church planters budget to buy new sound equipment and drapery, but used speakers, sound boards, pipe and drape, or even folding chairs or children's toys can save thousands of dollars. Every little bit can add up.

Host a 'baby shower'

Remember when you registered for your wedding or had a baby shower? Your friends were so excited that they threw a party for you and literally "showered" you with gifts and the things that you would need for this next season of life. You can do something similar for a church planter.

Have the church planter create a list of the things he needs: musical equipment, signage, office equipment, chairs, computers, etc. Then either the sending church can invite congregation members to pick something to purchase for the new plant or if there is a group of churches they can collaborate to buy individual items until those needs are met. This also has the added benefit of including your congregation in meeting those needs, making them feel more intimately connected and involved in the church plant's success.

Provide housing for the planter

The concept of a parsonage is diminishing in importance and value for pastors in the 21st century, but many older, established churches have one, and it often sits unused. Most church planters have a preparatory season in which they are raising support or planning for the plant, and free transitional housing could alleviate thousands of dollars of expenses over a year.

If you do not have a parsonage, you might have someone in

your church who has an extra property or Airbnb that could be used for the planter during this time. Money not spent on housing is money that can help planters reach their fundraising goals that much quicker.

Encourage support raising within your church

The bulk of a church planter's personal financial support comes from building a team of individuals who will contribute on a monthly basis for 3-4 years. It usually takes about 50-70 individuals to make up this support team and get the church planter over the crucial financial hurdle to work full time on the church while he plants without unnecessary distractions or part-time jobs.

This typically begins by the planter going to his close family and friends first, but soon their names will run out. If you will allow a planter to reach out to people in your church, that can be a significant boost to his fundraising efforts. Church planters can be coached to encourage potential donors not to shift their giving from your church to them, but instead pray about giving above and beyond their tithe. This mitigates any fear that a church planter would cannibalize from his partner church's budget.

Donate temporary staffing support

Do you have a staff member that could dedicate a few hours a week to help the planter for a year or two? Maybe you have a worship leader or children's ministry director who could use some of his or her time to help fill some volunteer gaps, build systems or policies or even help plan services. Even a few hours a week from an administrative assistant that has skills in accounting could be a huge help for a visionary church planter. Having experienced staff support is hard to come by in the early years of a church plant, which means having someone coming alongside to provide some assistance provides a significant amount of moral and operational support, and also frees up the church planter's time to recruit for longer-term roles.

Cover insurance

Getting insurance is a challenge these days. For pastors who are considered self-employed, it can be especially cost-prohibitive to get good insurance for himself and his family. You could free up thousands of dollars a year in health insurance costs if there is a way to add a planter to your group policy.

Capital campaign inclusion

As churches grow, they often do capital campaigns for building new buildings or expanding current facilities to accommodate new growth and vision. Churches often identify a missional need that a portion of the capital campaign goes toward — so adopt a church planter to support!

Choosing a church planter can actually be a significant encouragement to donors as they see their sacrifice not only meeting the immediate needs of the church, but also going toward something outside that impacts the kingdom. This can be a built in a way to cast vision for church planting and become generous toward a new church. If you don't have a church planter identified yet, consider creating a savings account for when that planter is identified.

Treasure and heart

Jesus often talks about money in the New Testament. In one of his most significant teachings, he says:

> "Do not lay up for yourselves treasures on earth, where moth and rust destroy and where thieves break in and steal, but lay up for yourselves treasures in heaven, where neither moth nor rust destroys and where thieves do not break in and steal. For where your treasure is, there your heart will be also." (Matt. 6:19-21)

Supporting the advancement of the kingdom through church

planting is an investment. It requires trust in the church planter, faith in God and a belief that God can and will advance his church beyond your local congregation. This vision and perspective of God's movement in the world is vital for all churches to succeed and thrive in the 21st century. Putting finances toward this vision requires faith, hope and lots of love for the kingdom of God, and established churches with resources and structure can be a crucial partner to advance church planting. But more than that, it also changes our churches and congregations just as much as it advances the church. Where your treasure is, there goes your heart, so place your treasure in the kingdom, and the heart of your church will follow.

Sending people and leaders

JOEL NELSON

Director of Church Expansion and Growth
for Converge North Central

God uniquely designed pastors to care for people. This is why one of the most predominant visual metaphors of pastoring in the Bible is a shepherd caring for his flock. Jesus describes himself as the Good Shepherd, laying his life down for the sheep. And for those with the gift of pastoring, truly investing in people and seeing them thrive is one of the greatest joys of ministry. But the beauty of this gift also has a shadow: the unique tension and pain when people leave.

We cannot talk about supporting church planting work without talking about sending people. And this can be one of the more challenging hurdles to overcome when supporting new works of the kingdom, even more than financial, but it is a vital one to address. The people who make up the launch team of a new work are extremely important, both volunteers and leaders. They are the ones who provide the backbone, infrastructure and support to the vision of the planter. With a healthy, robust, unified launch team, a church plant can thrive. Without a solid team, a church plant can fail even with the best financial resources and top-notch coaching.

A parent church is in the position to bless its daughter church by intentionally guiding and proactively helping the planter in building his very first (and perhaps most important) team. A good launch team that will leverage its strengths while balancing its weaknesses will multiply many times over the missional impact of the new church plant. A caring, well-established pastor knows his people's skills, weaknesses and giftings and can advise certain people toward jumping in. This also sends an undeniable message that your church supports the starting of new churches in every facet. It's a tangible way to exhibit generosity and faith, not just only in terms of the church budget, but also in terms of the people God has entrusted you with.

But sending people creates a tension within the heart of a good pastor who both loves his flock and also has a leading to help plant more churches. It can be hard to trust some of your congregation to someone else, especially someone who probably has stronger entrepreneurial skills than shepherding skills at this stage in his ministry. An important thing to remember in the midst of this tension is the words of the shepherd David:

"The earth is the LORD's and the fullness thereof, the world and those who dwell therein." (Ps. 24:1)

That last phrase is the game changer: "and those who dwell therein." Your people are God's, and he is their Ultimate Shepherd. As he calls you to step out in faith to support new churches, he will guide and direct his people to support that new work, and some of them may very well come from your own congregation. Having the perspective that everyone is the Lord's will help you navigate the complex waters of allowing a church planter to recruit from your congregation.

So, the question becomes: How do you, in wisdom and grace, determine to send people and leaders well?

To be clear: There is no universal answer here. A great deal depends upon the circumstances of the parent church as well as the church plant, but there are some guiding principles to consider and discuss among your team and the church planter you are supporting.

Determine the 'hunting license'

Part of parenting a new church involves allowing the planter to recruit from within the parent church(es). Prior to the actual recruiting, be as clear as possible about who can be recruited, how the church planter should recruit and how many people he can attempt to recruit. Many factors go into this. Are there other parent churches to recruit from? Will this require coordinating among multiple churches? How large is the parent church? What is the location of the plant in relation to the sending church? If there is a call letter or an expectation agreement between the parent church (or a group of parent churches) and the planter, include this number in the agreement.

Putting information down in writing will help both the church planter and the established pastor to determine clear boundaries. This will also benefit you both from overworking, causing confusion and unclarity when it comes to expectations. Mutually agree to go over a list of people prior to recruitment, agree to discuss how the church planter will be recruiting and clarify an estimation of how many families the church planter may take.

God is ultimately in control of who decides to come and who does not, and it is important to give the Holy Spirit ample room in the midst of this process to convict and call. However, you want to focus and hone the church planter's time and recruitment to key people who will be more inclined to jump in while avoiding those who will most likely stay at the parent church due to being on staff, key volunteers or those who have a vital role and significant investment in your established church. However, if that ministry leader, board chair or even the only drummer on your music team who can keep a beat comes to you saying they feel called to go with the new church, you should seek to help them discern that call and determine an exit strategy.

Keep gifting and personality in mind

In many ways, the characteristics of the launch team a planter recruits are reflective of what makes a good church planter. A well-rounded team should include people with various strengths like leadership, entrepreneurialism, faith, compassion, shepherding, teaching and evangelism. If everyone was like the church planter, then only a handful of things would be accomplished really well! A varied team can accomplish so much more.

Help a new planter in the recruitment stage by mapping out the personalities and gifting of potential people in your church. Seek to influence the planter to bring variety to his team. He might prefer and enjoy spending time with a specific type of person, but suggest balance and multiple giftings because a handful of key gifts might be overlooked, underserved or downright ignored. A sending church can help the planter by reminding the planter who he is and what kind of people he needs.

Quality before quantity

When I planted and we established the "hunting license" from our parent church, I had one couple in mind who were the same age as my wife and I and were active at our sending church. I mentioned their name to our lead pastor and he encouraged me to reach out to them. We had them over for dinner and my plan was to talk about the church plant, my vision and plan for the church, and invite them to consider joining our launch team. We did almost all of those things that night, but I never asked them to join us. Their car had barely pulled out of the driveway when my wife turned to me and inquired, "Why didn't you ask them?" I responded, "They just didn't seem like a good fit." I truly believed they were good people, but the more we talked with them, the more I felt they would have been great to be a part of the team, but not necessarily on the launch team right out of the gate. They would have "taken" more than they would have "given." I didn't want those distractions on the front end of our plant. And I'm glad I made that decision.

Having people is important, but having the right people is critical. Better to have 10 "sold-out" people than 100 passive observers. As you help sift through the people in your church and prayerfully determine who should be asked, seek to draw the best fits for the vision, not only the most talented leaders. When people are presented, challenge the planter by asking what he sees that person bringing to the launch team dynamics.

Observe second-tier leaders

There is no greater leadership incubator than a church plant simply because of the various needs that arise and the need for solid people to rise to the occasion and lead. In sending leaders, a good strategy is to identify those who aren't necessarily in a leadership role, but have exhibited potential to achieve greater and more influential leadership. Those in the wings have often been observing well-seasoned leaders ahead of them and they are simply lacking an opportunity to fully flex their spiritual gifts and passions. As an established church pastor of a sending church, ask yourself who might you see serving in a leadership role someday. Releasing them into the leadership needs of a church plant may be part of their growth process and journey toward maturity.

Understand the pros and cons of short-term

Often a part of the recruiting will include short-term volunteers or leaders to the launch team. Individuals will "sign up" for a specified period of time. In addition to providing critical mass, they bring leadership in some area from the very beginning with the task of building the ministry toward self-sustainability and raising up leaders. When this task is completed, they will be released to return to the sending church.

On the positive side, these people often bring energy, maturity and seasoned leadership to the new church. But challenges may come when they leave if they haven't fully completed the task, or it simply took longer to build a self-sustaining ministry and/or leadership. When key leaders leave, even if it is planned, their departure will always take some energy and momentum with them. There is no right or wrong way to go with short-term or longer-term commitments. It is simply important to recognize that short-term will often incentivize good leaders, but when they leave it will be difficult.

Remember agenda harmony

A sending church pastor is in the position to help the planter prepare for those important conversations with key people as well to help "vet" these potential launch team members. The preparation and conversations between pastor and planter are just as crucial as the meetings with the planter and the potential team members. Your role is to help the planter know exactly how he wants to communicate the foundational beliefs, values and strategies that will mark the new church's vision. The potential launch team members need to have a clear and comprehensive picture of what this plant is for, how it will accomplish the vision, and the methodology and how that might differ to what they're used to. All of those things are agenda harmony.

In one church plant, the planter recruited his launch team from his sending church and other supporting churches. On some crucial philosophical and polity issues, he was vague and never really defined them. He needed to build a team and he didn't want to lose quality people who had gifts, skills and passions to contribute to the team. When some of those philosophical and polity issues were pressed, he spoke with conviction as to his views and where he felt the new church should stand. The problem was, others who had been on the launch team had convictions that were different than the planter's and felt like they were the victims of a "bait and switch." The planter left the church soon after and the church limped along for a few years before closing. Not having agenda harmony has the potential to destroy the launch team.

Help provide agenda harmony among the people who are being recruited, those who have signed up, and the planter. A sending pastor can be a crucial clarifier and sounding board to help his people see the vision, join the vision and have agenda harmony among the team. Remember, this is not your church plant, but God's and the vision of the planter. Your job isn't as much to influence and dictate the vision as it is to clarify and promote the vision among key people in your church.

Loving enough to send

Pastors are built to love and care for their people. And, as we mentioned at the beginning of the chapter, it is difficult to entrust the people you love to someone else. But remember this: It is loving and caring to send people toward a church plant. Like parents encouraging their children to strike out on their own, oftentimes the only way people can grow is if they leave and form new bonds under a new vision. You can play a key role in their story, but remember, your people's story doesn't stop with you.

You are simply part of a long line of churches going back thousands of years that have sought to expand the kingdom of God by starting new churches. There are costs — financial resources, time, emotional energy and also by sending people you truly love to advance the global church.

But God promises a reward for your sacrifices:

"Give, and it will be given to you. Good measure, pressed down, shaken together, running over, will be put into your lap. For with the measure you use it will be measured back to you." (Luke 6:38)

Challenge the people in your church to be a part of this new plant as a part of their discipleship and serving pathway. Model the faith you want to see in your church planter by remembering that everything is God's, nothing and no one is yours to keep, and that by giving your leadership away, you're joining in the global work of God, who doesn't just send resources, he sends people!

Partnering with others to plant churches

JEFF GAUSS

Church Planter

"Two are better than one, because they have a good reward for their toil. For if they fall, one will lift up his fellow.
But woe to him who is alone when he falls and has not
another to lift him up!" (Eccles. 4:9-10)

In the Garden of Eden, God made it crystal clear we were not
meant to be alone. He designed Adam to long for a partner, someone to come with him on the journey to care for creation and see
the world thrive. And since the fall, one of the key agents of the
enemy of God is to get us alone and isolated to keep us from being
effective in the calling God has for us. And isolation is a great hindrance to effective and impactful church planting.

In Converge, we say "we are better together," and that is especially true when considering supporting and establishing church plants. In 2012, I was part of a group of pastors in rural Minnesota called a LEAD team. This group gathered quarterly to learn together, encourage one another, achieve initiatives together that couldn't be accomplished alone and dream together about reaching the entire region with the good news of Jesus Christ. I began to share a vision about us collaborating together for church planting and got some immediate pushback.

Years after successfully planting churches through this LEAD team, a pastor named Bob approached me and said:

"You know…uh…I think I need to repent. When you started talking to our group about planting churches several years ago, I scoffed in my heart. *Why do we need more churches?* I thought. I mean, my own church is struggling. We should help the ones we already have instead of starting new ones. I didn't have a very good attitude about it. But I see now how God uses new churches to reach new people, and I just wanted to say, 'I'm sorry I was so critical.'"

Unfortunately, Bob's attitude toward church planting is quite common, especially in rural areas where pastors and churches often see church plants as a threat rather than an opportunity. It is perceived that people are a commodity to be stored, and they are always at a premium in the rural areas I have pastored in. There are real fears that a shiny new church will steal people from their already resource-deprived congregation and the natural inclination is to protect your territory. The supernatural reaction is to expand your territory by partnering with others to start new churches to reach the unreached.

Here are four commonly held myths about partnering together in planting churches that we need to overcome to truly work together.

Myth 1: Your church needs to be a certain size

Many churches think that planting churches is something that only large churches can do. This is partially true. Only large churches can plant churches alone, but churches of any size can plant churches together. Ten churches of 100 people can partner together to plant churches just like one church of 1000 can. I would even argue that a church planted by multiple churches will be stronger and healthier than the church planted by just one. It takes a diversity of involvement and shared ownership to plant with a team, and a major benefit is that an established church doesn't have to be a certain size to partner in church planting. I've seen churches with less than 20 people get on board with church planting and support a church planter as a local missionary. It's the size of your vision, not the size of your congregation, that matters.

Myth 2: Your church needs to have a certain amount of money

True, it does take a sizeable amount of money to fund a new church plant. This is even more reason to partner with other churches! The financial burden is distributed among many churches instead of falling on the shoulders of just one. Plus, there are many ways an established church can give to church planting other than from the general budget.

We discussed the specifics of this in Chapter 6, but as a reminder, multiple churches together can strategize to do some or all of the following and have major impact in the life of a church plant:

> **Special offering:** Invite the church planter to come and share during your worship service and take a special offering for the church plant or to support the planter. If four churches are partnering together, this can add up to a great amount!

Personal support: Give the church planter a "hunting license" (discussed in the previous chapter) specifically for financial requests of individuals within your church. Oftentimes this actually garners more support for the planter than a one-time gift or special offering without taking anything away from the church budget.

Joint fundraisers: Organize a joint fundraiser between partner churches to help support the church plant. This could be coupled with a joint church "shower" (discussed in Chapter 6), which would be able to build relationships across churches together for a common goal. Also, it is always a bonus if it involves the church planter in a dunk tank!

Special projects: If a church plant is local or regional to your partnership churches, send people to help with an outreach event or child care for launch team meetings. You will be surprised how far people will drive to do a one-time event that they believe will have a true impact. I have heard of multiple churches donating child care services for launch team meetings or even the first few months of a church plant after launch.

There are many ways churches of any size can partner in planting churches. No contribution is insignificant. Again, it's not the size of your budget, but the size of your vision that matters.

Myth 3: Your church needs to be healthy first

Church health is unquestionably important. We want every church to be a beacon of health and vitality. But let's face it, there are a lot of stagnate, dying and dysfunctional churches out there. And a lot of the reason they are so unhealthy is because they don't have a kingdom mindset. They've entered self-preservation mode. The mission has ceased being about reaching others with the good news of

Jesus Christ and has become about just keeping the lights on.

The best cure for entropy is exercise. You don't get healthy by lamenting how unhealthy you are. You make the journey toward wholeness by taking action, one step at a time. We looked at some research in Chapter 1 that demonstrated churches that partner in church planting begin to see revitalization themselves. Attendance, giving, salvations and baptisms all tend to increase when an established church is involved in church planting.[1] It may seem counterintuitive, but being involved in church planting can help an unhealthy church get healthy as its people see real life change taking place in the church plant and begin to believe that it could also happen in their own context.

Myth 4: A new church will steal people from your church

This is a fear that we have already addressed, but it is probably one of the greatest hindrances to established churches partnering together to plant churches, especially ones in their "backyard." The reality is that the average new church gains 60-80% of its new members from people who are not attending a church; whereas, churches over 10-15 years of age gain 80-90% of new members by transfer from other congregations.[2] This means that an established church is actually much more likely to "steal" people from an existing congregation than is a church plant. Church plants tend to reach people who aren't and won't be reached by the current church landscape. As a result, the conversion and baptism rate in a church plant is much higher.[3]

That said, a new church plant needs mature believers to help reach unbelievers, and multiple churches partnering together can send less people per church and yet have the same impact as sending more people from one church. This means that even smaller churches can send someone to join a launch team and still have a combined impact that is greater than simply working alone.

Moving from myths to partnerships through relationships

Pastor Bob believed these myths, which is why he was initially so defensive. But God used our LEAD team working together over time to change his mind. Remember, this team gathered quarterly to learn together, encourage one another, achieve initiatives together that couldn't be accomplished alone and dream together about reaching the entire region with the good news of Jesus Christ. Regardless of whether you have a team, loose network or formal association, spending consistent and intentional time together with other pastors is where collaboration moves from conversation to concrete practice.

How you spend time with other pastors is key to building partnerships that have weight and influence. Here are some practical "how-tos" for partnering with other churches to plant churches:

Build the relationship

Pastor Bob's attitude didn't change overnight. It came as the result of years of building into the relationship. One thing we consistently did was **play together.** Men typically build relationships by accomplishing something together and/or competing against one another. It's always a bonus if it's fun and laughter is involved. Go fishing, golfing or hunting together. Go to sporting events and/or play sports together. Get the families together and grill out. Recreation breaks down barriers in ways that work never will. We had fun and built lots of trust along the way.

Another thing we did was **pray together.** Prayer isn't just about sharing our heart with God; it's about sharing our heart with each other. In prayer, our deepest hurts, desires and dreams are revealed — and shared. It's really hard to be mad or critical of someone who just prayed fervently for your struggling family. Prayer draws our hearts closer to God and one another, and it helped unify us under a common compassion for one another as we interceded for our city together.

We also relentlessly **supported one another.** As a church planter, it's easy to come off as smug to other pastors. After all, we're starting a new church because we think there is something missing in the community that we can provide. The best way to counter this preconception is to privately and publicly support other pastors and churches. Sharing their events on Facebook, praising them from the pulpit and encouraging them in their ministry was an essential precursor to partnership. When we have personally been validated, we naturally want to validate others.

Cast a kingdom vision

Part of spending time together involved pastors from different church contexts and sizes sharing stories of life change in their church with the other pastors. This was not in the vein of bragging (which is often the perception), but as a way of inspiring one another. Once people began to see God moving outside of their immediate context, it began to inspire a kingdom imagination for what could be. We began to dream together. What if God did what he's doing here in the town where our children go to college? Or the next community over that doesn't have a gospel-centered witness? Or in your own church?

Vision is compelling and contagious. Converse with other pastors about where they see a need for the gospel. Strategize together about what it would take to meet that need. And then dream together about what it would do for the community if that need were met. Ownership in the vision creates excitement, responsibility and accountability. Churches that are involved in the process will be hard-pressed not to be involved in the solution.

Celebrate everyone's contribution

In our partnership we had churches that contributed anywhere from $1,000 to $120,000 to our church planting fund (see Chapter 6 for more info on this). They contributed at varying levels depending on the size and health of their church, but everyone contributed because everyone owned the vision, including Pastor Bob. And we celebrated everyone the same, no matter what level they contributed at. This was a win for the team, not for any individual. So, I went and spoke at each and every church and personally thanked and celebrated their contribution. In fact, the smallest contributor was the farthest away. It cost me half of their contribution in travel expenses, but it was worth it. Why? Because we were the first church plant they had ever supported in their 110-year history. That's worth celebrating!

When we celebrate everyone's contribution equally, we validate the truth that absolutely every church can partner in church planting, no matter its size or budget. And when churches feel that their contribution is meaningful, they are likely to contribute again. And when they contribute again, they are likely to make partnering in church planting a habit. And when it becomes a habit, it's on its way to becoming a church culture-changing value. And when church planting becomes a part of the culture, churches move from being a contributor to being a catalyst in church planting. Every step on this path is cause for celebration!

Partnering together produces lasting contribution

Partnering together with other established churches to plant removes the excuses of size, finances, health and people. It introduces a new paradigm into the mix, one where any church can come together with others to be the church a church planter needs. This can create lasting connections among established churches that come together for a common vision outside of themselves, and can help revive dying churches to a renewed vision and focus.

And whatever happened to Pastor Bob? He's now an elder in my church plant! After years of talking about church planting and seeing its effectiveness, he decided he wanted to be a part of one. Such is the case when we let go of our natural inclination to protect and defend, and partner with others to expand kingdom territory and ignite a movement in our midst.

9

The life cycle
of healthy
planting

JOSHUA YOUNG

Church Planter and Lead Pastor
of Redeeming Hope

"Behold, children are a heritage from the LORD, the fruit
of the womb a reward. Like arrows in the hand of a war-
rior are the children of one's youth. Blessed is the man
who fills his quiver with them!" (Psalm 127:3-5a)

As the psalmist so aptly describes, children create a legacy and
that legacy is worth celebrating and enjoying. Arrows were useful
tools in ancient Israel for protecting and also hunting to provide
food for the family. A skillful archer would use his arrows well, and
keep a healthy amount in reserve for emergencies. The analogy of
children to such a tool of war and provision was striking, and still
is today.

As we have been exploring, planting a church from an established church is much like parenting a child. Your involvement has a rhythm and a life cycle and one thing is absolutely certain: Your role will change. It cannot be a strict, linear or mechanical formula that is followed the same way every time, but there are discernable patterns of the life cycle of healthy parenting that we can extrapolate and highlight for planting from an established church. And just like a healthy family, your plant should mature and grow more independent from its sending church(es) over time. Within the right framework that balances framework and freedom, they should begin to stand on their own, branch out, come into their own, and then impact their world in ways you never could.

However, there is always a danger to be overbearing and controlling. In parenting, this results in children either clinging to their parents or resenting them, and in planting this can be the same result. Plants can rely too heavily on their mother church and become a drain on financial or relational resources to the point of unhealth. Or an overbearing coach can push his plant away, breaking the bonds of brotherhood and mutual ministry and creating a negative experience that can damage the plant, your church and possibly prevent others from supporting a plant in the future.

If parenting is done well, daughter churches can truly be a joy to their mother church and a testimony to the faithfulness of the Lord and the advancement of his church. They can also be a continuation of a legacy, which means your church can have a lasting influence and create generations of Jesus-followers. But it takes recognizing your role, where and when to lean in or pull back, and selflessly focusing on the planter's health and growth above what he can or should be doing for you. As a mentor of mine once said: "be careful to love people fiercely, but hold them loosely." Here's a guide on the life cycle of planting and how you can lead well in each stage.

Conception + pregnancy

Initially the seed of an idea begins to grow in your midst to plant a church. This is a beautiful and exciting time as God raises up leaders and begins to bring people to the forefront. As we have discussed, this idea might have been catalyzed by you (or a team of pastors), or you might have had a planter already come to you with this idea. Regardless, the Lord is the one who gave the vision. This conception of an idea is great in the beginning, but if you have ever seen a pregnant woman at seven months, the giddiness and excitement wear off. During the development and pregnancy phase, things begin to get tougher, because you have the excitement of vision, but maybe developmental needs, funding or the right team is delaying the birth. This is all normal and, just like a baby, churches need TIME to grow and develop to become healthy enough to bring this stage to completion.

As an established church pastor who is coaching and guiding this process, anticipate frustration and a longing to "just get it done." Don't move too quickly to solve problems, but provide godly wisdom and counsel, and practice temperance and restraint. Consider yourself like a good husband supporting his pregnant wife, provide practically and keep the stress at a minimum. Continue to encourage the planter to feed himself and his forming church family with gospel truth, don't become too eager to jump ahead but don't be timid when the time comes to launch. Like a family that "nests," encourage the planter to prepare for the birth/launch well (good structure, healthy culture, intentional discipleship, leadership development, outreach-focused). Your involvement is crucial, but remember, you are not the planter. As we have discussed in previous chapters, let the planter lead the vision. You are a facilitator, guide, sounding board and mentor.

Birth + celebration

The birth of a church is a chaotic, frenzied and fantastic time. People are getting excited, the date is set, and the plans are made to see this vision become reality right in front of your eyes. During this stage, it can be easy to be distracted by the small things. Like a soon-to-be first-time mom trying to find the "right" music to play during the birth, planters can be distracted and overemphasize small things.

Your role here is to celebrate this amazing milestone and encourage the planter to focus on the big picture. Remind them to pray, read the Bible consistently, still take a day off (even leading up to launch Sunday!), and remember that what you do in the beginning will be easier to continue. In this stage, seek to provide helpful leaders and calm leadership. Don't over-reach and control, but be the sounding board and the safe person for the planter to trust. Let him wrestle through the pains of birth, and remember that every hiccup and difficulty is being used by God to grow the planter in front of you. In the midst of celebration, let Deuteronomy 6:6-7 be your drumbeat:

> "And these words that I command you today shall be on your heart. You shall teach them diligently to your children, and shall talk of them when you sit in your house, and when you walk by the way, and when you lie down, and when you rise."

Whatever happens leading up to or on launch Sunday, celebrate and remind them that their identity and value is in Jesus and his work for them.

The terrible twos

The first year of a plant is filled with constant readjustments, growth or decline week by week, lots of challenges and (like parenting) sleepless nights. It is a blur. In that first year, check up on the spiritual health and vitality of the church planter more than anything else. Most often God is using the challenges and celebrations in the first year to grow the planter more than the plant, just as parenting sanctifies the parents more than the children. They need to be consistently fed on the Word, and the challenges are like learning to crawl and speak, they are being prepared for greater achievements in the future.

Around year two, anticipate disruption and challenges that will require a more directive and careful leadership. As we addressed in Chapter 5, a planter will almost always face a financial, personal and leadership crisis within the first two years. It is here that your input will be crucial. Godly reminders won't be enough; give clear input on their personal walk with Jesus. Encourage them to pray more than talk. Read the Bible in personal devotions and listen in fervent prayer more than externally processing and trying to strategize their way out of difficult circumstances. Leaders who leave need to be encouraged and cared for, not looked at as enemies or deserters. All of this requires grace.

Also, in this time, make sure their finances are taken care of. It might not be best to back off financial support in years 2-3 if possible. These seasons can make or break a church plant, and you want to be the stable and involved parent church that keeps them safe and focused.

Adolescence + forming

But, like any season, the terrible twos will pass and the church will continue to mature. It is the freedom and the stretching that come in years 3-4 that can make or break your personal relationship with your church plant. As things become more stable, more people and leaders come and the church moves toward self-sustaining, this is where the good planter begins to shine and his unique perspectives on ministry and mission come to the forefront.

It is here that it is important to remember that this is the planter's vision and God's vision, not yours. They might establish leadership structures different than you would, or utilize resources in a different capacity than you, and that is OK. Leaning in and attempting to control will only push them away. Your role should move into advisor, friend and resource. Help remind them of the vision, keep them focused on balancing development (of the believers in their midst) with mission (reaching out to more people). Begin to encourage them to work toward multiplication.

This is where your experience as an established pastor can help contribute to healthy rhythms in their life and ministry. Most planters love the thrill of the new and want to keep reinventing the wheel. Gently caution them in this and help guide them from planter to pastor. Keep the friendship going, and don't push too much. Let the wise words of Paul to the Colossians guide your relationship with the planter: "Fathers, do not provoke your children, lest they become discouraged." (Col. 3:21)

Maturity + mentorship

As the church plant comes into its own, the planter becomes an established church pastor like you. When the plant moves to become self-governing, self-sustaining and self-propagating, this is where your role can change again. Like parents with grown children who begin their careers, approach this relationship like a mentor. You know the planter/pastor's tendencies, strengths and hang-ups. Use that knowledge to install an impulse for renewed multiplication and a continued legacy.

Renewed multiplication

How many times have you heard (or said) of parents to grown children, "When am I going to get a grandchild"? That's a beautiful impulse to keep the family going, and grandchildren are loads of fun to play with and then return to their parents! Keep the planter-now-pastor focused on multiplying out, and start to encourage grand-plants. Stay out of the individual weeds of specific situations in the church, but gently encourage on a broader level toward multiplication through the plant.

This season has helped you and your church recover from the effort and energy of planting directly, while also keeping it going through the daughter church. You want the planter to become the established church pastor who plants. Establishing a mentor (parent to adult child) relationship can be helpful in influencing toward a renewed focus on multiplication.

Continued legacy

Once you see the maturity of an established church coming from your midst, it is not time to rest on your laurels. As grandparents have significant influence in the lives of their grandkids, you still have work to do to influence toward kingdom multiplication. Being a mentor to a granddaughter church and working together can be a huge help to your initial church planter and also begin to establish legacy and regional influence. Your role can look like Paul's instruction to Titus:

> "Likewise, urge the younger men to be self-controlled. Show yourself in all respects to be a model of good works, and in your teaching show integrity, dignity, and sound speech that cannot be condemned, so that an opponent may be put to shame, having nothing evil to say about us." (Titus 2:6-8)

Also, planting again should not be out of the question. Abraham had a child in his old age, and you can have multiple children and grandchildren at the same time. Keep the drive alive, because the kingdom needs mature, godly, established church pastors with financial and spiritual maturity to catalyze the church and multiply it across a region.

From vision to legacy

Billy Graham once said: "The greatest legacy one can pass on to one's children and grandchildren is not money or other material things accumulated in one's life, but rather a legacy of character and faith." Your faith, faithfulness and steadfastness to be a good parent can influence generations of church plants. Vision is necessary, but legacy stands the test of time. To move to legacy, it takes significant investment and sacrifice, and especially wisdom in how to handle each stage of a daughter church's life cycle. Too much or too little involvement can be unhelpful and unnecessary, but a balanced, helpful, fatherly approach can truly stand the test of time.

Commit to parent and grandparent well. Doing this will influence mature, godly *generations* of churches and church planters that collectively advance the kingdom in ways that one church simply could not. This is how the church has stood up to the gates of hell for 2000 years and boldly proclaimed: *not today!*

10

Common mistakes when church planting

NATE HETTINGA

Church Planter

Most churches struggle to multiply not because of a lack of vision, a lack of desire or a lack of kingdom-mindedness, but because it's HARD! Having kids is always complicated, and the first one is always the scariest. My wife and I have six children and at times have described our first-born as the "practice child." Honestly, we really didn't know what we were doing when the hospital foolishly sent us home with this tiny little eternal soul and said, "Good luck!"

Parenting is daunting, but good parents learn from the wisdom and the mistakes of others. We also study our own upbringing and decide what to eliminate and what to maximize from our experience of being parented, and we read, learn and grow to be the best parents we can be. Rick Warren wrote in *The Purpose Driven Life:* "We are products of our past, but we don't have to be prisoners of it."[1]

Planting demands creative flexibility in order to meet the changing cultures and generations represented in our communities. While no one template will adequately cover every scenario, some principles can be identified that seem to be constant. The following are some common mistakes I've made and/or seen others experience and all of these lessons have been learned the hard way:

Not structuring long-term for multiplication

Without a mission for multiplication at every level in your church, you can be consumed with your own congregation's issues and lose sight of what gives people life in the first place. Churches that don't structure and sacrifice to plant other churches will soon find themselves old and sterile.

If you are going to be serious about church planting for the long haul, losing leaders is a critical factor to consider when planting. Key leaders leave to plant, and we have seen sending churches often scrambling to fill the holes or even close down specific ministries for a bit while in "recovery." In our context now, every hire is a potential planter or plant team member and each key ministry leader is strongly encouraged to bring up others to either take over ministry or be planted into ministry. In some seasons, this has worked really well for us, and when a daughter church is launched, a full team of trained leaders is ready to go.

Underestimating the sacrifice of multiplication

We have often seen established churches that are surprised by the financial and leadership sacrifice that comes from intentional multiplication. This has stopped some partnerships dead in their tracks, or caused some churches to pull back after committing because of the strain it causes. Here are some ways to mitigate the sacrifices of planting specifically as it relates to finances and leadership:

Finances

Our church began by giving 10% of every dollar from our general offerings to church planting (here, near and far). After about 10 years, we moved the needle to sacrificing 20% to the same missional focus. And that hurt. We chose to live on less so that others can simply live — for eternity. That means that we are constantly building a planting "war chest" so that when opportunities for multiplication arise, we're already prepared and mitigating the financial hit.

Serious commitment to planting churches is expensive. A solid slice of the budget bottom line must be carved out and protected for church planting.

Leadership

When leaders leave it always hurts. After 33 years of ministry and 23 years of pastoring a plant, I still feel the loss of every leadership family that chooses to step out into mission. The crazy thing is, encouraging planting is my fault — I want my church to plant, but whenever we do, I lose friends via proximity and passion.

Here is an interesting truth: Leaders seldom leave well. Like an adolescent leaving home, they have to be critical enough of their parents to be convinced that they can go do it themselves and they're usually pretty sure they'll do it better. That's a good thing, but it's a tension to be managed, not a problem to be solved. Often, planters or key leaders will come back and apologize at some point for how they left home. And let's be honest, some of us have had to do that with our own parents too. Anticipating this tension on the front end will mitigate personal hurt when leaders leave more vocally than you would like.

Forgetting to celebrate multiplication well

What we celebrate tends to get repeated, and it is tempting to celebrate internal wins because it keeps people committed to the vision of your church and serving in your context. But talking about multiplication from the platform, making a big deal out of churches that are born (network-wide), giving updates from plants, and praying for more plants will keep this in front of your people.

When multiplication isn't put forward consistently, it will become foreign to your people and they won't understand or get excited about a multiplicative vision when it is presented. To offset this risk, put daughter churches on stage and give them the mic for a few weeks. I've told our church, "Listen well to this guy and ask the Lord, 'Am I called to go?'" The permission of the lead pastor matters. Your congregation wants to know if it is OK for them to leave home and start a new work.

Not anticipating the 'how long' and the 'who' of coaching

In the early years of our church plant, I paid close attention to the church planting material available and remained focused on reaching unchurched people, yet, as the needs of the growing church expanded, I became preoccupied with management detail and lost the outward drive that had sustained our early growth. We planted churches and led people to Christ, but were not positioned primarily to make a difference by serving the needs in our community. A coach is necessary beyond the three-year mark to help keep "first things first" and challenge the planter to fight the inertia that seems to plague any growing organization. I wasn't prepared for this long-term investment at first.

It is also important to remember the type of coaching that is needed. A coach should be focused on the success of the planter and the new church, but a mother church pastor is split: He's trying to support the planter who is building a new flock while also protecting his own. Both sorts of oversight are necessary, but it might not always be wise for them to be embodied in the same individual. We finally learned this lesson while sending out church No. 4 and hired a coach to mentor the planter.

Creative church planting requires long-term funding

We planted churches in prisons and cross-culturally to Spanish-speaking people and both required ongoing financial support beyond the three-year support cycle we usually follow. There is no magic way to "fix" this situation (if it even needs to be "fixed"), but in the case of cross-cultural ministry, it may be prudent to start the work with a bi-vocational planter or one who is better equipped to subsist on the salary available from an impoverished fellowship.

Ignoring your gut and your leadership

Church planting is exciting, addicting and intense. For an entrepreneur, it's a rush unlike no other, and at times it can be tempting to rush ahead and ignore warning signs because the urgency of a need seems too great to wait. The Holy Spirit is faithful to provide prompts that should be heeded, regardless of the needs that seem to be pressing at the time. Every time I've ignored a sense of unease about a planter or strategy, it's come back to haunt us.

The lead pastor, elder team and key staff also have a responsibility to guard the value of missional ministry and balance that with what the church needs (not in fear, but in faithful dependence on God). The cost is too high and the pain too great for anyone else to attempt to drive ahead when circumstances scream "pull over, this is killing us!"

Shortchanging assessment

It can be tempting to avoid the cost and time of assessment, especially if you seem to have an amazing leader in front of you. This is especially difficult when a church planter has a good track record, multiple ministry experiences and previous assessments. It might feel right in the moment to move on ahead. But, even if a planter has been assessed in the past, reassessment for the plant proposal at hand is crucial. What made a church planter a good fit in urban Philadelphia might make him fall flat on his face in rural

Minnesota. When we didn't do this, it proved costly both financially and relationally.

In addition, we've learned to pay close attention to the issues addressed by the assessment process. Follow-up is key, and even more difficult when the pressing needs of building a team and raising support are at play. Thinking that we know the person or the situation better and can eschew his portfolio is a mistake. Assessment is not God's final word on an individual, but it's an amazingly accurate predictor of outcomes and pitfalls. As Proverbs 11:14 says: "Where there is no guidance, a people falls, but in an abundance of counselors there is safety."

Inflexibility on philosophy or strategy

I have seen established church pastors try to look for a younger version of themselves to plant out, but each generation requires that fresh strategies be employed to communicate the good news. Some creative ideas will fail and you can mutter, "I told you so," but others will win the lost and you'll soon be employing them in your own context. Encourage creative missional engagement relentlessly with every plant and seek diversity of philosophy, not homogeneity.

And while it's good to have a plan, somehow I don't think that the Holy Spirit is a "systems guy." Many daughter churches will follow a template and a strategic plan, but some will just sort of pop up as opportunities. Learn to keep one eye always looking for the next multiplication win, even if it comes from unlikely places. That youth pastor who got kicked out of his church for talking about planting (it happens)? Grab him and see if there's a fit. That independent plant about to launch? Adopt them, coach them, fund them. Be open and avoid the trap of inflexibility.

Unclear expectations

What will the mother church contribute? What will she not be able to give/do? Church planters are notorious for taking as much as they can get (that's what I did), and mistrust or rankled relationships can easily develop when details are not clearly spelled out in writing and signed by both parties. Provide written, documented clarity and you will avoid this major pitfall.

Working and visioning alone

Trying to plant by yourself is an unnecessary challenge. The churches of our planting family have formed a network that meets for several hours once a month. We dream, strategize and pray together about the future of our multiplication movement. The most striking example of partnering is visualized when a new plant requires funding, and we raise much of the money by polling the pastors at the table.

Take every chance to talk about the value of multiplication and the central place it has in the life of your congregation. Eventually, it can become part of the culture of the church so that it is natural to think of going or giving to new churches.

Rushing planters out the door too soon

We need to value bringing planters into our church to let them absorb the DNA of our context. Planters will learn to love the people and be loved in return. Let them start a ministry with the safety net of the mother ready to catch any failures. Give relentless but caring feedback that is designed to strengthen leadership and character traits.

The planter should also have the opportunity to teach within the mother church (student ministry, men's, college age, etc.) on a periodic basis. In addition, we give our multiplication leaders a three-week sermon series close to their launch date. The congregation is encouraged to consider, "Could I listen to the dude for the next 10 years?"

Serving alongside of others for a season also encourages the planter to form partnerships and recruit people on the launch team that balance his weaknesses with the strengths of others.

Even if the team members are volunteers or bi-vocational, they are in place and able to multiply ministry much more effectively as the church grows.

Not praying enough

Churches and leaders often give lip service to this value, but fail to practice it with fervency. Techniques do not multiply churches; God does. When Christian leaders ask the Master to do what he has already said he wants to do he clears the obstacles and the church flourishes.

As I said at the top, my wife and I have six children. I know, that's a lot! And we've made a TON of mistakes in the parenting process over almost three decades. But there is no greater joy for us as parents than to see our kids walking with Jesus, starting their own families and growing the next generation. Our hope is that they will learn from our mistakes, count the cost and keep reproducing! Avoid or mitigate some of these mistakes in your context as you seek to be faithful to the call of God to plant churches.

11

Planning for recovery and reproduction

PAUL ROOT

Associate Minister of Church Planting,
Converge PacWest

"If you wait until you are ready to have kids, you'll never have 'em."
– Everyone

My wife (Theresa) and I were married for five years without kids. We were waiting until I finished my master's degree to start a family, but this situation created a few comical scenarios. One of these was when I was serving as a director of a training program for pastors in northwest Mexico. One day one of these pastors called me and said, "I have a young lady in my congregation who is unmarried and pregnant. She would like to put the baby up for adoption, and I wondered if you and your wife would be interested in adopting the baby?"

I quickly figured out that my friend assumed that because Theresa and I had been married five years and didn't have children, that we were biologically unable to. He expected that we would have grown our family by now, and was lovingly giving us an opportunity to have a child by adoption.

Two years into my church plant near San Francisco, one of my best launch team members came to me and said, "This experience on our launch team has awakened a call in my heart to plant a church, to reach a large population of people in Silicon Valley who speak my language but don't know Christ." We didn't feel prepared to plant again; our own church was still forming and solidifying! But we listened to the call of God and sent him out, and he planted two more churches!

Shouldn't it be our "natural expectation" that as a church or church plant, we should reproduce ourselves multiple times over? When church planters are recruited within our network, they have written expectations that they will plant again or be significantly involved in helping another new church start. I believe my friend in Mexico was right. It is normal and healthy to reproduce, and churches align with God's mission and advance his kingdom when we plant new churches. I long to see multi-level reproduction be the cultural norm for our network of churches and church plants.

But how do we get ready to plant again? Just like having a baby, planting again doesn't happen immediately or automatically. It takes time to prayerfully recover and rest, discover and rediscover God's unique vision for a new plant, and then get everyone on board with a new vision to plant again. Here are some strategic steps you can do to plan for recovery and reproduction:

Celebrate the win of planting

People thrive off of seeing "wins" and how their hard work has advanced the kingdom of God. It actually meets a deep need in the human heart for significance, value and lasting impact. Visionaries struggle with celebration because, once they "take the hill," there are always five more on the horizon they need to rush toward. Once your church has planted, celebrate that win early, often and in multiple ways. Don't let it be forgotten or diminished. Honor specific milestones in your church plant's life and keep bringing updates from the planter in front of your people.

This celebration is key to your church's recovery and future reproduction. As you communicate the significance of this in the life of your church, it both feeds the need for recognition but also feeds the desire to do it again. Remember, visionaries will more quickly get on board with a new plant faster than "late adopters." Take your time to celebrate and you will earn the relational capital to plant again.

Pray about the next opportunity

Jesus had an overwhelming compassion for lost people. Matthew gives us an inside look at Jesus' heart:

> "When he saw the crowds, he had compassion for them, because they were harassed and helpless, like sheep without a shepherd. Then he said to his disciples, 'The harvest is plentiful, but the laborers are few; therefore pray earnestly to the Lord of the harvest to send out laborers into his harvest.'" (Matt. 9:36-38)

His first response to this compassion was to turn to his disciples and tell them to pray. And this is an expectant prayer that God is going to unfold his plan to raise up more workers for this labor. Here are some good prayers for you and your church to pray in the recovery phase:

- *"Guide us to be refreshed by your love and rejoice in your work."*
- *"Deepen our love for you and willingness to follow, wherever and however you lead."*
- *"Help us be filled with the same compassion and courage of*

Jesus to boldly love the lost."
- *"Use us to identify and raise up workers for the harvest field."*
- *"Help us see that the work of the kingdom is not done, but it is only beginning."*

As you pray these prayers, you are acknowledging your deep need for God's grace. It is humility that drives us toward prayer, and engaging with Jesus in this way will bring healing, restoration and recovery to your church and your people.

Keep moving out into the harvest

Ministry in an established church almost always has a gravitational pull inward. A launch team member came to me nine months into our launch and said, "Paul, all this evangelism we've been doing has been exciting and fruitful, but it's exhausting! Don't you think we should back off and focus on helping these people grow?" We quickly get inwardly focused and forget that there's a ripe harvest field God has called us to work in.

Be intentional about getting out and building meaningful relationships with lost people in your community. This can start with initiating conversations with people in your neighborhood, volunteering in your community or simply hosting a party to rub shoulders with people who do not yet know Jesus.[1] As you are impacted by these conversations and gospel engagements, share stories with the people in your congregation. This reminds them that their work is not done, even if you have already planted. The Great Commission is an equal opportunity employer!

Rediscover your community's 'lostness'

You might have been so focused on the plant that your immediate community took a back burner. A great way to recover is by rediscovering the lostness of your community and the beauty of Jesus to meet that lostness with his grace. Whatever stories people share in your community demonstrate their hopes, dreams and idols. What questions are people asking? How are they hurting, lost and harassed, like sheep without a shepherd?

Focusing on the mission field in which God has placed your church keeps the *missio dei* alive post-planting. This action also requires you and your congregation to be out and listening to your community, which connects with the previous step. Host prayer and discovery sessions with key leaders to do the hard work of rediscovering the right vision for your community.

What if we knew our community's pulse so well that people walk away from conversations thinking: *They really get me.*

Leverage church planting strategies in your context

I've learned so much from my son-in-law when we go fly fishing together. The best time to fish is when the fish are hungry, early morning and just before sunset when they strike at the bugs landing on the water's surface. We experiment with all kinds of flies to find out what attracts them. We find specific places and settings where trout congregate and travel. You can say I've gotten "hooked" on fly fishing!

As my son-in-law has shared his passion and strategies for catching fish, so we must learn from our church planters and integrate their strategies in our context. Let the church plant be the R&D for implementing new ways to reach people in your established church context. This keeps things fresh and allows you to learn from those you send out.

Anticipate partnerships and planting again

Don't think, "We might plant again." Resolve that "we *must* plant again." There are people who are lost, harassed and helpless, like sheep without a shepherd. Begin to go back to the initial stages of hunting for a vision and a planter. You will be shocked at what expectant faith will do!

Partnering with your daughter church is another step toward

reproduction. Planting is fresh in their minds and hearts, and already ingrained in their culture from the get-go. Maybe offer a collaborative partnership with your daughter church to plant another church together. Bringing the planter on as an equal collaborator can strengthen the bonds of your two churches and create a kingdom-mindedness that can help begin to reach an entire region for the gospel.

As we consider recovery and reproduction, it's important to remember Jesus' top priority was connecting with and reaching lost people. He loved them. He spent time with them. And he said: "There will be more joy in heaven over one sinner who repents than over ninety-nine righteous persons who need no repentance." (Luke 15:7)

- As you recover, pray.
- As you rediscover, prepare.
- As you reproduce, praise.

We all get to be on this mission, and we get to be on it with the Author of Life. Jesus loves us, he equips us and he sends us to join with his Holy Spirit to produce the impossible. And in the words of Paul, let's stay the course and...

"Let us not grow weary of doing good, for in due season we will reap, if we do not give up." (Gal. 6:9)

Afterword

LEE STEPHENSON

Our family moved from Mesa, Arizona, to Orlando, Florida, in the spring of 2015. That was one of the most challenging decisions we have ever made. Mesa truly was home. We started a church in 2009 and over the years saw the power of the gospel change many families and individuals. We built a home in the dream community where we lived next door to the park, and our kids had more friends to play with than one could imagine. Years later, I still find myself trying to explain to people why we left our family and our church in Arizona we so dearly cherished. My simple answer to that question is we knew God was — and is still — in it with us.

In my role with Converge, I have a unique opportunity to travel around our country and to some pretty uncommon places internationally to meet with pastors and church leaders. Something I see over and over, and that comes up in conversation routinely is that we live in a world that is working to drown out God's voice. We see the media, news, politicians, magazines and places of education all working overtime to drown out God's voice. People are more medicated than dedicated. People are walking through their days in drudgery, believing they aren't good enough. If people don't know what God really has to say and what he believes about them, it is easy and convenient to believe the lies of the enemy.

This is why we have to commit to go. We can't say "No," when God says "Go!" And yet, if you are anything like me, we can be really good at coming up with excuses for why we can't go. Trust me; I have tried. When confronted with the idea and opportunity to move to Florida, I tried to say no. We were good. The church we planted was firing on all cylinders. Why would we leave now? I didn't even know anyone in Orlando. I thought it would be a nightmare because everyone would want to stay with us so they could have a free place to lay their heads when they visited Mickey's house.

Most of us share the same struggles. What is this going to cost me? I am not smart enough. I don't have the right leaders or enough money in the bank. Our excuses easily become constantly loud: I can't, I can't, I can't, and I don't, I don't, I don't.

But have you ever thought about the ramifications if we say "no" or if we say "yes" to going?

In Deuteronomy 1, we find a similar moment taking place. God is working through Moses to challenge his people one more time. Moses is now face to face with a new generation. This generation has known nothing besides what it looks like to live in the desert wilderness. They grew up hearing stories of God leading the people out of Egypt. They grew up on the edge of the promised land, being able to peer in but never able to enter. They knew that the 11-day journey their parents and grandparents were supposed to take ended in living out their remaining years, 40 in all, in the wilderness not getting to enter into the promised land. What was supposed to take 11 days turned into 40 years.

I wonder how much of our Christianity gets lived out right here. What should have taken 11 days turns into 40 years. We find ourselves doing laps around the same old mountain and addressing the same old issues:

- Nobody is going to buy into that vision.
- We have never done it that way before.
- How do we get more people giving?
- How do we get more people serving?
- Is it even possible to reach non-Christians in this community?

Pastors and leaders, we are guilty of this in our own lives. We keep walking around the same mountains dealing with our past, our issues and our insecurities. And as a result, a journey that should have taken 11 days turns into 40 years. What is your 40 years (personally or even in your church)? What are the same old mountains that keep getting circled?

I believe God is saying to some pastors, leaders and churches, "You have been here long enough!"

Sure, there have been some remarkable moments in recent church history. We have seen God use the Calvary church movement in the 1960s. We witnessed the rise of the megachurch with mega ministries. We recently saw the Vineyard movement take off. These have been some incredible wins and reminders of what God can do and is even willing to do. At the same time, we have seen some losses from the previous generations. We have witnessed churches get overly focused on church growth and as a result forgetting what it meant to make disciples. We have seen churches turn inward and lose sight of evangelism and the call to simply share Jesus.

What we must recognize is that every new generation presents a new opportunity. We can admire the faith and work of the past, but we can never claim it as our own. We must be prepared to live it ourselves.

As Deuteronomy 1 plays out, God steps into the picture 40 years later and says, "Hey! You have been here long enough."

And now the generation is standing in the same spot as the previous generation and the question is whether or not they will repeat the same mistake. The future nation of Israel found themselves in a moment where they were challenged to break camp and advance. God disrupts their normal. For all of us, there are moments in our journey that God steps in and disrupts our normal and says, "It is time to change." These moments happen on our faith journey but also in the lives of our churches. God has something new, and to experience the new, we have to be willing to break free from the old and move and advance toward the unknown.

To break camp and advance after 40 years required a major change in their mindset. The longer you stay somewhere, the more comfortable and connected you become. It is harder to want and accept change. God reminded his people they weren't home yet, and they needed to shake off their settledness and move.

At the end of Chapter 1, Moses reminds the people of what happened with the last generation. He sent 12 leaders to go and spy out the land that God had told them he was going to give them. Ten of those leaders came back with a negative report and declared there was no way that they could win and go in. Joshua and Caleb were the only men to come back and say, We can do this! God is with us, and he is giving us this land. We have nothing to fear because God has not given us a spirit of fear. Wherever we go, we have the opportunity to see the world transformed through the power of God. Just 10 people coming back with a negative report had the power to change an entire generation's destiny.

What we do matters! What we teach, blog, post, tweet matters. Are you a part of the negative naysayers, the doom and gloom conversation, or are you a part of the conversation that is life-giving and inspires hope, love and opportunity?

We, too, have this moment in history and in our nation. The church can change the narrative. That is why we took the effort to put this resource together. I believe that God is telling us a group of churches that the time is NOW! More church planting is needed. God has set the land before you, and it is time to break camp and advance.

What is God calling you to do? Honestly, I can't answer that question for you. All I can say is that we need:

- more engaged churches willing to go to a new land
- more people that are willing to go
- more churches and individuals willing to sacrifice more
- more ways of getting the job done
- to be more reliant on God's power

What I know and what I decided a long time ago is that when God says, "GO!" I don't want to say, "NO." Are you with me?

Notes

Chapter 1: Why church planting matters

[1] Farmer, Jeffery (2007). *Church planting sponsorship: a statistical analysis of sponsoring a church plant as a means of revitalization of the sponsor church* (Ph.D. dissertation). Information retrieved from WorldCat Database in May 2019. (OCLC No. 229121490).

[2] Additional information from Dr. Farmer's presentation, a presentation of his methods, and this partial list of his extensive findings can be found here: <https://caskeycenter.files.wordpress.com/2017/05/church-revitalization-through-church-planting-sponsorship-powerpoint.pdf>

[3] Matt. 19:29-30, 25:14-29; Luke 14:10-11

[4] Eph. 5:22-29 (a body of parts); 1 Cor. 12:27 and Matthew 12:49 (part of family); Eph. 2:19 (a living home or temple); 1 Peter 2:5 (living stones)

[5] Herron, Fred. *Expanding God's Kingdom through Church Planting.* (Lincoln, Neb.: iUniverse, Inc. 2003), 19.

[6] Eph. 1:22-23; 1 Cor. 15:9

[7] Wagner, C. Peter. *Church Planting for a Greater Harvest: A Comprehensive Guide.* (Ventura, CA: Regal Books, 1990).

[8] "The vigorous, continual planting of new congregations is the single most crucial strategy for (1) the numerical growth of the body of Christ in a city and (2) the continual corporate renewal and revival of the existing churches in a city. Nothing else — not crusades, outreach programs, parachurch ministries, growing megachurches, congregational consulting, nor church renewal processes — will have the consistent impact of dynamic, extensive church planting." Keller, Tim. *Why Plant Churches* <http://download.redeemer.com/pdf/learn/resources/Why_Plant_Churches-Keller.pdf>

[9] Stetzer, Ed. *Christians in the Age of Outrage.* (Carol Stream, IL: Tyndale Momentum, 2018), 170.

[10] Lyle Schaller, quoted in D. McGavran and G. Hunter, *Church Growth: Strategies That Work.* (Nashville: Abingdon, 1980), 100. See also C. Kirk Hadaway, *New Churches and Church Growth in the Southern Baptist Convention.* (Nashville: Broadman, 1987).

Chapter 2: Interceding for the impossible

[1] Billheimer, Paul. *Destined for the Throne: How Spiritual Warfare Prepares the Bride of Christ for Her Eternal Destiny.* (Grand Rapids, MI: Baker Publishing, 1975).

[2] Bounds, E.M. *Purpose in Prayer.* (New Kensington, PA: Whitaker House Publishing, 2011).

Chapter 8: Partnering with others to plant churches

[1] Farmer, Jeffery (2007). *Church planting sponsorship: a statistical analysis of sponsoring a church plant as a means of revitalization of the sponsor church* (Ph.D. dissertation). Information retrieved from WorldCat Database in May 2019. (OCLC No. 229121490).

[2] Donald McGavran and George Hunter, *Church Growth: Strategies that Work* (Nashville: Abingdon, 1980), 100.

[3] See: David T. Olson. *The American Church in Crisis* (Zondervan, 2008) and Ed Stetzer and Warren Bird. *Viral Church* (Jossey-Bass, 2010), 25.

Chapter 10: Common mistakes when church planting

[1] Warren, Rick, *The Purpose Driven Life: What on Earth Am I Here for?* (Grand Rapids, MI: Zondervan, 2002).

Chapter 11: Planning for recovery and reproduction

[1] A great book to help you get out there is *Neighborhood Mapping: How To Make Your Church Invaluable To the Community* by Dr. John Fuder.

ㅓ CONVERGE

Converge is a movement of churches working to help people meet, know and follow Jesus. We do this by starting and strengthening churches together worldwide.

For over 165 years we've helped churches like yours bring life change to communities in the U.S. and around the world through church planting and discipleship multiplication, leadership training and coaching, and global missions.

We're committed to starting missionally minded churches until every people group and community has heard the gospel. We start churches that start churches to see lives changed with Christ's love and truth. Converge provides a clear pathway for you to plant a new church, campus or to multiply your church. We've created proven strategies, systems and training all designed to improve your success so that more people will have the opportunity to accept Jesus.

If you're ready to launch a new church or campus, Converge has already created a proven pathway you can implement now. Rather than committing your own resources (time, money, people) on developing church planting or multiplication systems, we can partner with you to start more healthy congregations. Our expertise in church planter assessment, coaching, funding strategies and church residencies to raise up new leaders can help you multiply faster. As partners on the same mission, we're more effective working together to reach more people with the gospel.

Connect with us at churchplanting@converge.org or 800.323.4215 to learn more.